EDGAR RICE BURROUGHS'

Tarzan®

THE JOE KUBERT YEARS

Volume One

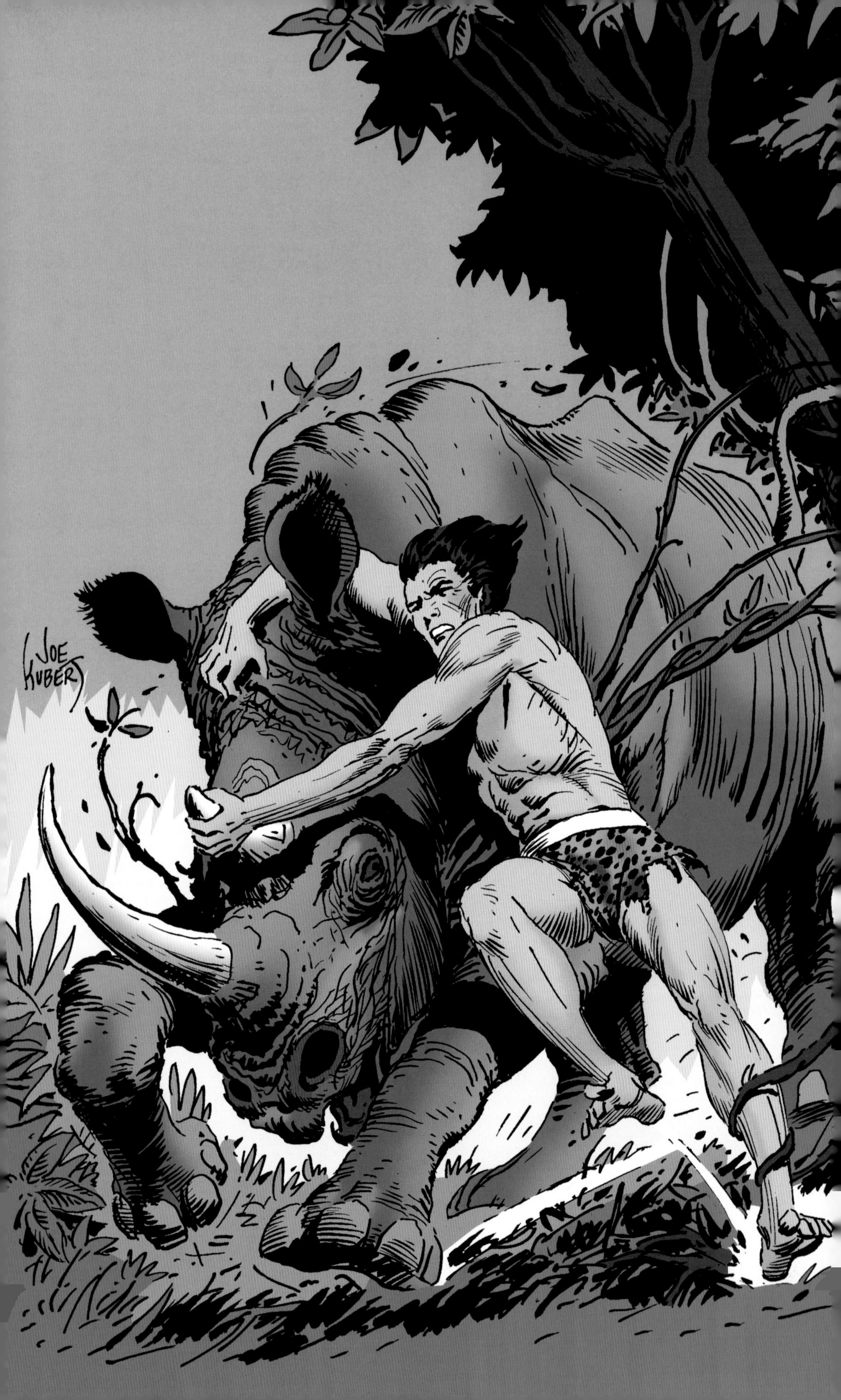
JOE KUBERT

EDGAR RICE BURROUGHS'
Tarzan
THE JOE KUBERT YEARS

Volume One

WRITTEN AND ILLUSTRATED BY
Joe Kubert

TM
DARK HORSE BOOKS™

PUBLISHER
Mike Richardson

ORIGINAL SERIES EDITOR
Joe Kubert

COLLECTION EDITOR
Philip Simon

COLLECTION DESIGNER
Joshua Elliott

ART DIRECTOR
Lia Ribacchi

DIGITAL RESTORATION
Sno Cone Studios

SPECIAL THANKS TO DANTON BURROUGHS AND SANDRA GALFAS AT EDGAR RICE BURROUGHS, INC.,
ROGER BONAS, PETE CARLSSON, SHELLEY EIBER, AND ADAM KUBERT.

Published by
Dark Horse Books
A division of Dark Horse Comics, Inc.

Dark Horse Comics, Inc.
10956 SE Main Street
Milwaukie, Oregon 97222

www.darkhorse.com

To find a comic shop in your area, call the
Comic Shop Locator Service: (888) 266-4226

First Edition: October 2005
ISBN: 1-59307-404-2

3 5 7 9 10 8 6 4 2

Printed in China

TABLE OF CONTENTS

**ALL STORIES WRITTEN FOR COMICS, ILLUSTRATED, AND LETTERED
BY JOE KUBERT, EXCEPT WHERE INDICATED
ALL COVERS BY JOE KUBERT
ORIGINAL COLORS BY TATJANA WOOD**

INTRODUCTION
by Joe Kubert

My earliest memory of the birth of my love for cartoons and comic strips was reading Edgar Rice Burroughs' *Tarzan*, as illustrated by Hal Foster. The syndicated strip appeared in the *New York Mirror*, a tabloid-size newspaper in the early 1930s. *Tarzan* was always printed on the back page of the comics section, taking up that full page in color. The strip was not published as a daily. It was only on Sunday that the *magic* appeared.

I've been drawing since I was old enough to hold a pencil (or a piece of chalk). My predilection in subject matter was for "muscle guys." And, like most youngsters starting to draw and just beginning to understand anatomy, proportions, and perspective, the figures I drew were exaggerated. Muscles were popping out of every conceivable place. Muscles on top of muscles.

But, in reading Foster's *Tarzan*, I recognized a salient fact and an important lesson.

Here, in these beautifully rendered yet deceptively simple drawings, Tarzan, the Ape-Man, became a living, breathing entity. The figures were real and alive. And the credibility of characters and background transported a kid living on Sutter Avenue in East New York Brooklyn into the mysterious green and vibrant world of the African jungles.

When Tarzan fought the gorilla who had slain his father, I could literally feel the powerful blows on the man's skin and the painful rent of the beast's tooth and nail. When the huge black-maned lion challenged the Lord of the Jungle, I could feel the strength of the Ape-Man's legs circle the great cat's body, while he drove his blade again and again into the raging beast's heart. The ability with which Hal Foster was able to engender that sense of total realism and believability was magic.

Jump ahead with me now some forty or fifty years later. I've been a professional cartoonist from the age of eleven, and I've had the good fortune of working with some wonderful writers. People like Bill Finger, who wrote some of my early *Hawkman* stories. Gardner Fox, who scripted the *Flash* and any number of other comic-book characters. And, of course, Bob Kanigher, editor

and author of *Sgt. Rock* and so many titles too numerous to mention.

As a result of a request from my good friend and then publisher, Carmine Infantino, I became an editor at DC Comics, with my responsibilities including the war books, covers, and as many *Sgt. Rock* stories as I had time to do.

One bright, sunny day, Carmine called me into his office. "Joe," he said with a broad smile, "how would you like to do *Tarzan*?" Carmine and I had known each other since we started in this business. If anyone knew of my love for Burroughs' *Tarzan*, he did.

I jumped at it.

Here was an opportunity for me to connect again with the joys of my childhood. To infuse myself into the world of Tarzan, the Ape-Man, and to write and draw the character that had been an inspiration to me.

First, I re-read all the *Tarzan* novels. This was step one in re-acquainting myself with the origin. Then, I studied Foster's work, some of which I had never seen before. I learned that *Tarzan* first appeared in newspapers as a series of captioned illustrations rather than sequential panels. In fact, Foster never included balloons for dialogue in either *Tarzan* or in his later work, *Prince Valiant*. My intent in doing *Tarzan* was to inject the excitement and immediacy that I felt when I read *Tarzan* for the very first time. I made every effort to recapture the reality that was so pervasive to me.

The experience of doing these books you now hold in your hands was an unrivaled joy, and I'm grateful that Dark Horse has decided to republish my work in this form.

I hope you enjoy my efforts, and if you decide to pick up the original novels by Edgar Rice Burroughs for the first time (or to read them again), I'll have accomplished my goal.

Joe Kubert
Dover, New Jersey
April 15, 2005

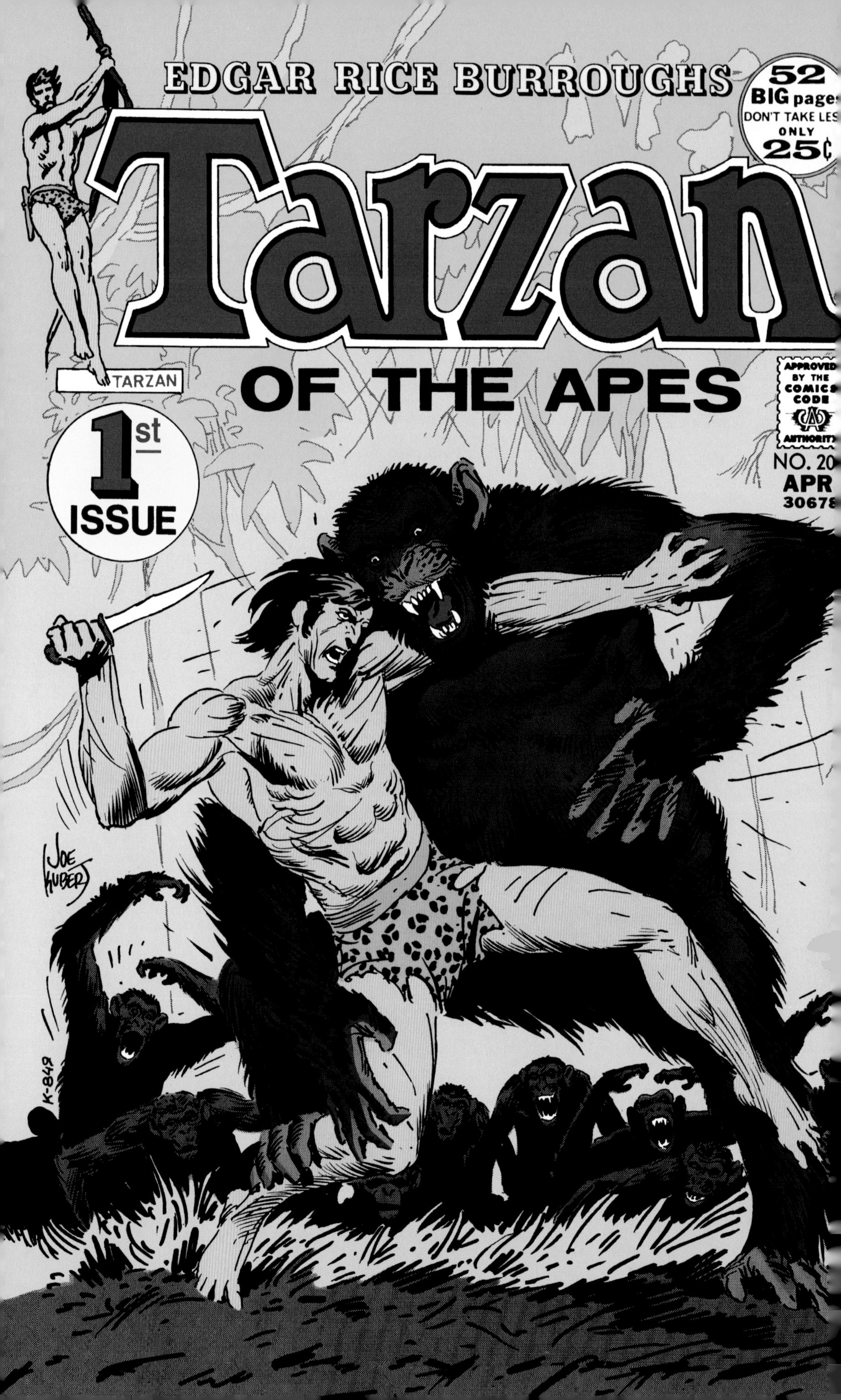
EDGAR RICE BURROUGHS
52
BIG page
DON'T TAKE LES
ONLY
25¢
TARZAN
TARZAN
OF THE APES
APPROVED BY THE COMICS CODE AUTHORITY
1st ISSUE
NO. 20
APR
JOE KUBERT
K-849

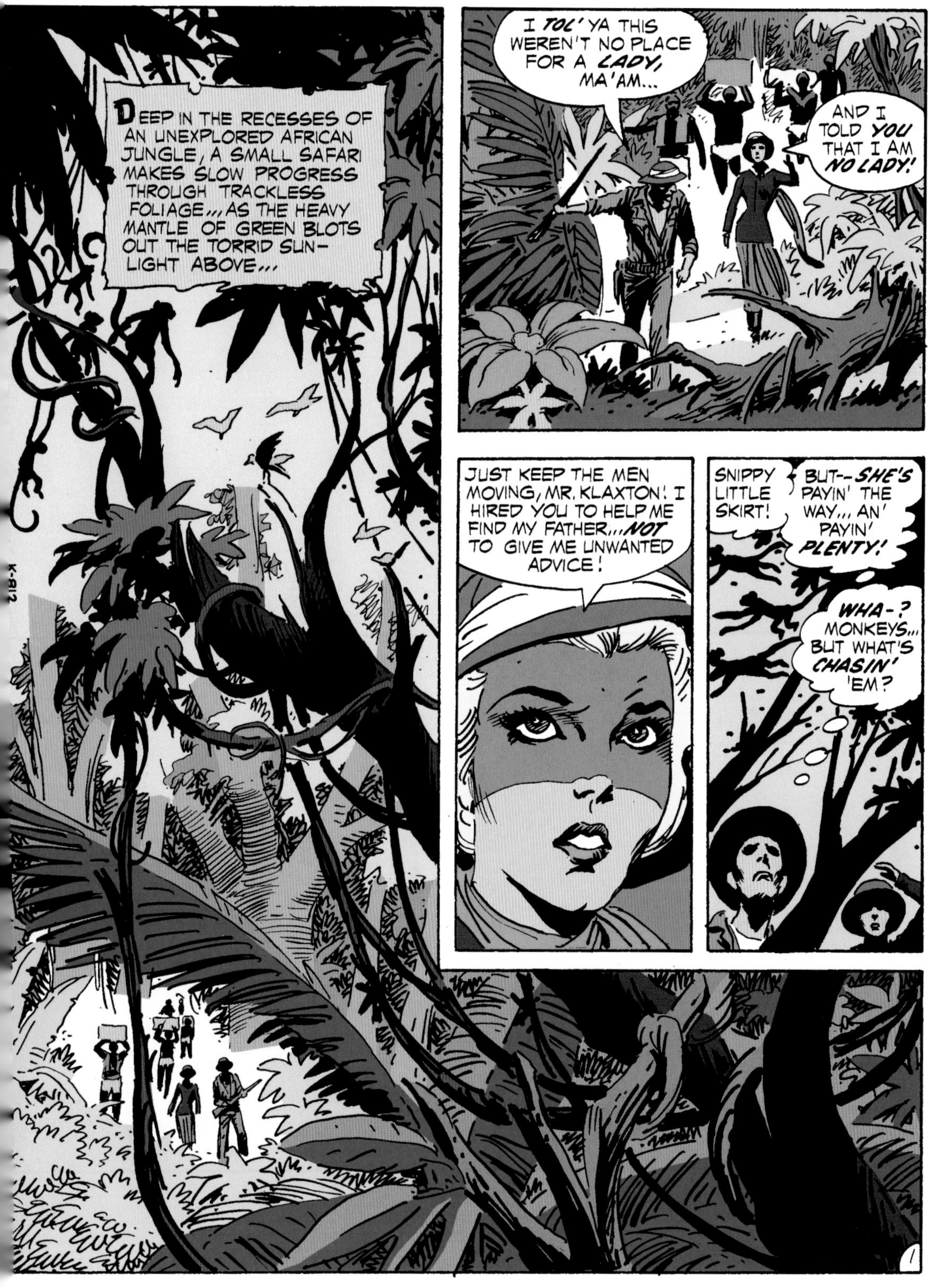
DEEP IN THE RECESSES OF AN UNEXPLORED AFRICAN JUNGLE, A SMALL SAFARI MAKES SLOW PROGRESS THROUGH TRACKLESS FOLIAGE,,, AS THE HEAVY MANTLE OF GREEN BLOTS OUT THE TORRID SUN-LIGHT ABOVE...
K-812
I TOL' YA THIS WEREN'T NO PLACE FOR A LADY, MA'AM...
AND I TOLD YOU THAT I AM NO LADY!
JUST KEEP THE MEN MOVING, MR. KLAXTON! I HIRED YOU TO HELP ME FIND MY FATHER... NOT TO GIVE ME UNWANTED ADVICE!
SNIPPY LITTLE SKIRT!
BUT--SHE'S PAYIN' THE WAY... AN' PAYIN' PLENTY!
WHA-? MONKEYS... BUT WHAT'S CHASIN' 'EM?
1

PANTHER! GIT DOWN, MA'AM!

HYPNOTIZED BY THE HORROR AND FEROCITY OF THE SCENE BEFORE HER EYES, THE YOUNG GIRL CANNOT MOVE... AS THE TWO PRIMORDIAL FORCES MEET.... *IN A CONTEST TO THE* **DEATH!**

SUDDENLY...THE UNMISTAKABLE CRY OF THE *BULL APE* ECHOES AND RE-ECHOES THROUGH THE THICK FOREST...

AS IF STOPPED BY AN ELECTRIC CURRENT, THE GREAT SHINING CAT STOPS IN MID-CHARGE...

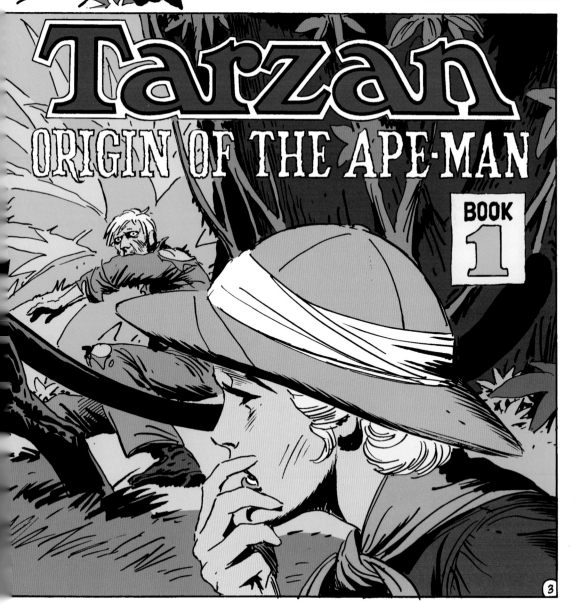

Tarzan
ORIGIN OF THE APE-MAN

BOOK 1

3

LOCKED TIGHT IN COMBAT, BEAST AND MAN-BEAST WHIRL AND ROLL ON THE JUNGLE FLOOR....

MUSCLE AND SINEW STAND OUT AGAINST WHITE SKIN AND INK-BLACK FUR....AS DULL SUNLIGHT GLINTS OFF HONED STEEL....

THE KNIFE ARCS AGAIN AND AGAIN....BLOOD FOLLOWS THE BLURRED PATH OF THE STRIKING BLADE....

NOW THE MAN STANDS ASTRIDE THE FALLEN BEAST.... AND ONCE MORE A BLOOD-CHILLING CRY ISSUES FORTH! *THE VICTORY CRY OF THE GREAT BULL APE.*

BEFORE THE SAFARI CAN RECOVER, THE MAN IS *GONE!* MELTING BACK INTO THE DARK, BLUE-GREEN JUNGLE.... WITHOUT HAVING SAID A WORD!

WH-WHO.... WAS.... THAT...?

I'VE--HEARD TELL OF AN *APE MAN*...BUT--I NEVER BELIEVED... HE ACTUALLY *EXISTED!*

AN *APE MAN?*

LISTEN HERE, MISS, WHEN YOU HIRED ME TO FIND YOUR *FATHER* IN THIS FORSAKEN PLACE...I *DIDN'T* AGREE TO FACE UP TO NO *WILD MAN!*

BUT, PERHAPS.... HE *KNOWS* OF MY FATHER'S WHEREABOUTS? WHY NOT ASK--

YER DAFT!

I'VE HEARD TELL THAT... *THING*... HAD A *APE* FOR A *MOTHER!*

HERE'S THE STORY.... LIKE *I* HEARD IT...

ORIGIN OF Tarzan OF THE APES

*T*HE YEAR IS *1888*... PORT OF *DOVER, ENGLAND*... A SHIP LEAVES FOR FREEPORT, ON THE AFRICAN COAST....

ON BOARD, JOHN CLAYTON (*LORD GREYSTOKE*) ACCOMPANIED BY HIS WIFE, LADY ALICE.... SETS OUT ON A MISSION OF STATE FOR HER MAJESTY, THE QUEEN....

OH, JOHN.... OUR SOJOURN TO AFRICA WILL BE LIKE A *SECOND HONEYMOON* FOR US!

YES, ALICE...

*L*ATER, IN FREEPORT....

WE WISH TRANSPORT TO THE BRITISH WEST COAST!

ARE YOU AVAILABLE?

AYE! ME SHIP AN' CREW BOTH! FER A *FEE!*

THAT CAPTAIN FAIR GIVES ME THE *SHIVERS*, JOHN!

'TIS TRUE, ALICE...I'LL NOT BE UNHAPPY WHEN WE PART WITH *HIS* COMPANY!

5

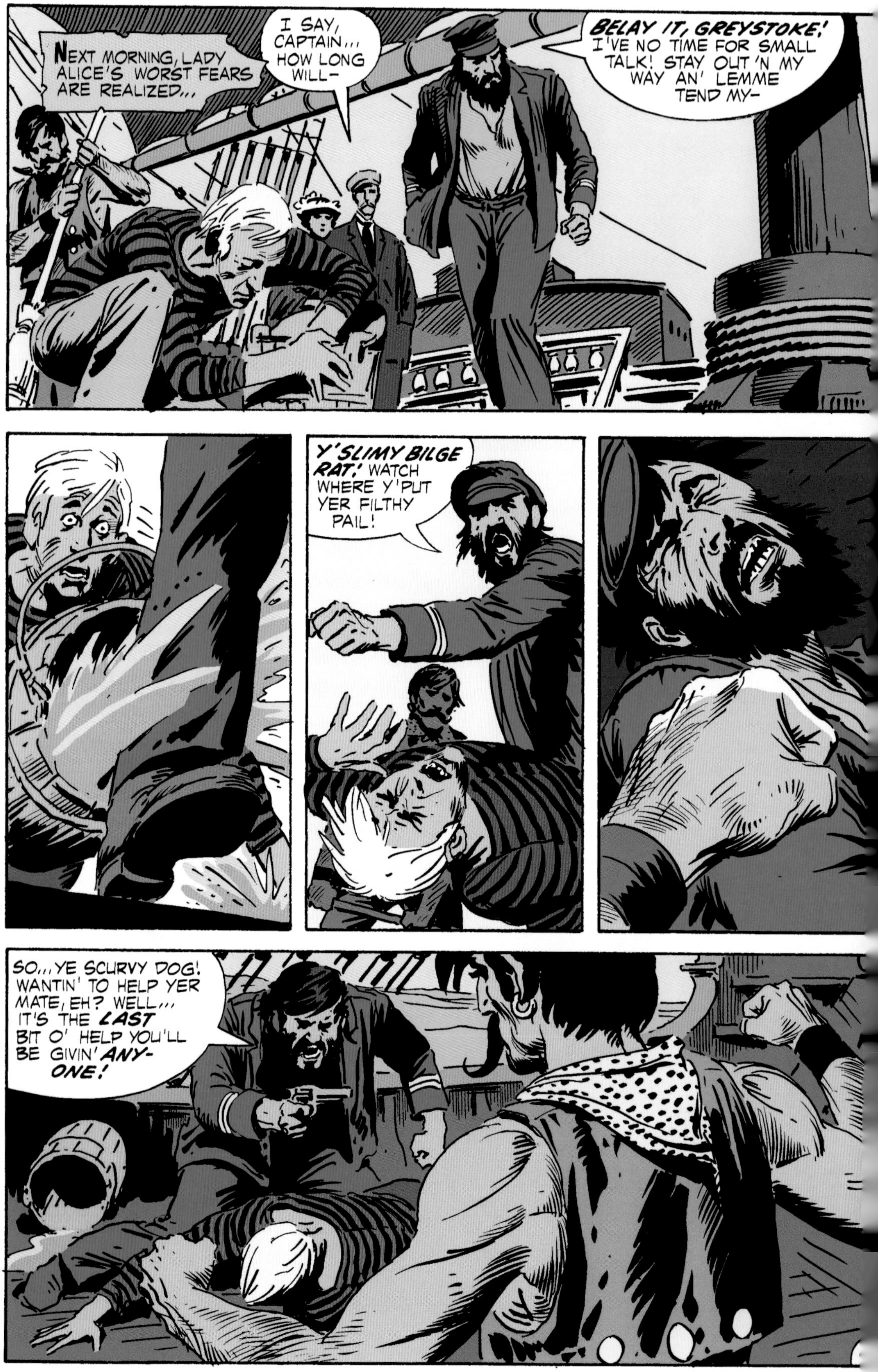
NEXT MORNING, LADY ALICE'S WORST FEARS ARE REALIZED...
I SAY, CAPTAIN... HOW LONG WILL-
BELAY IT, GREYSTOKE! I'VE NO TIME FOR SMALL TALK! STAY OUT 'N MY WAY AN' LEMME TEND MY-
Y'SLIMY BILGE RAT! WATCH WHERE Y'PUT YER FILTHY PAIL!
SO... YE SCURVY DOG! WANTIN' TO HELP YER MATE, EH? WELL... IT'S THE LAST BIT O' HELP YOU'LL BE GIVIN' ANY-ONE!

NOW, NOW, CAPTAIN... YOU WOULDN'T *KILL* A MAN.. MERELY BECAUSE HE *JOSTLED* YOU A BIT!

GET BELOW, YOU TWO!

YE CAN THANK THIS GENTLEMAN FER SAVIN' YER WORTHLESS LIVES!

BLACK MICHAEL THANKS YE, SOR...

AND SO, THE *FUWALDA* SAILS ON...WHILE SEETHING HATE AND VIOLENCE THREATENS TO ERUPT FROM THE SHIP'S BOWELS...

AS LORD AND LADY GREYSTOKE ASCEND THE SHIP'S STAIRWAY NEXT MORNING...

P-PLEASE, SIR... *DON'T* GO ABOVE DECKS! THERE'S... *TROUBLE!*

STEPPING TOPSIDE, A WILD SCENE GREETS THE GREYSTOKES... A SCENE OF *BLOODY MUTINY!*

NONSENSE, MAN! THOUGH I APPRECIATE YOUR SOLICITUDE, NEVERTHELESS!

ARMED WITH BOATHOOKS, AXES AND CROWBARS, THE CREW OVERWHELMS THE SHIP'S OFFICERS....

HERE'S *TWO MORE* FER TH' FISHES! *HEE-HEEE*--

THOSE TWO ARE *MY FRIENDS!* ANYBODY TOUCHES THEM'LL DEAL WITH *BLACK MICHAEL!*

D'YA HEAR?

FOLLOWING THE MUTINY,,, AND THE **MURDER** OF ALL SHIP'S OFFICERS,,, THE **FUWALDA** TACKS CLOSER TO THE AFRICAN JUNGLE COAST,,,

I'LL HAVE TO LAND YOU AN' THE MISSUS ASHORE,,,

FOR I FEAR I **CANNOT** CONTAIN THE CREW FROM DOIN' YE HARM!

PUT US OFF,,, **HERE** ,,, IN THIS **WILDER- NESS?**,,,

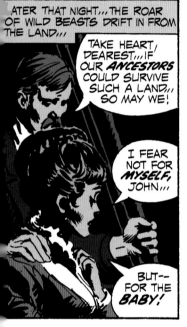

LATER THAT NIGHT,,, THE ROAR OF WILD BEASTS DRIFT IN FROM THE LAND,,,

TAKE HEART, DEAREST,,,,IF OUR **ANCESTORS** COULD SURVIVE SUCH A LAND,,, SO MAY WE!

I FEAR NOT FOR **MYSELF,** JOHN,,,

BUT-- FOR THE **BABY!**

I-I KNOW! BUT--PERHAPS WITH THE HELP OF PROVIDENCE,,,ANOTHER SHIP WILL FIND US-- **BEFORE** IT IS BORN!

DAWN OF THE FOLLOWING MORNING,,, IN A SMALL HIDDEN LAND-LOCKED HARBOR,,,

ALL YOUR BAGGAGE,,, AND SOME FOOD STORES,,, WILL BE LEFT WITH YOU!

I WILL GET WORD TO THE ADMIRALTY! A SHIP WILL BE SENT,,, BEFORE LONG,,,

BLACK MICHAEL'S FALSE PROMISE RINGS IN THEIR EARS, AS LORD AND LADY GREYSTOKE WATCH THE LONG BOAT'S DEPARTURE,,,

NEITHER KNOWS THAT THIS WILL BE THE **LAST TIME** THEY WILL EVER SEE ANOTHER **HUMAN BEING!**

9

NOW FOR THE FIRST TIME... THE FULL IMPACT OF THEIR SITUATION CAUSES LADY ALICE TO TREMBLE...

OH, JOHN... I-I'M SO *FRIGHTENED!*

YOU'VE BEEN SO BRAVE, MY DEAR...

DON'T GIVE IN NOW!

NOT THE SECOND HONEYMOON WE ENVISIONED, 'TIS TRUE... BUT-- WE WILL MAKE THE BEST OF IT!

CHOOSING FOUR STOUT TREES LORD GREYSTOKE BEGINS TO CONSTRUCT A SHELTER...

IT IS FORTUNAT[E] THAT BLAC[K] MICHAEL LEF[T] US *ROPE*... AN *AXE*... AND *FIREARM[S]*.

WE SHALL BE *SAFE* ON THIS RAISED PLATFORM... ABOVE THE GROUND!

LISTEN TO THE MONKEYS CHATTER...

...AS IF THEY OBJECT TO OUR INVADING THEIR DOMAIN!

AS THE EARLY NIGHT'S DARKNESS SLOWLY SETTLES...

JOHN...! WHAT IS... *THAT?*

WHAT... *WAS* IT?

I... DON'T KNOW, M[Y] DEAR! PERHAPS... A MERE SHADOW!

LET US GO TO SLEEP!

18

A BLOOD-RED TROPICAL MOON CASTS AN EERIE GLOW AS THE TWO BONE-WEARY CASTAWAYS FALL INTO A DEEP SLUMBER...

THE GREAT CAT SNIFFS AND CLAWS AT THE SHELTER SUPPORTS...

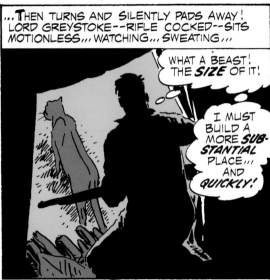

...THEN TURNS AND SILENTLY PADS AWAY! LORD GREYSTOKE--RIFLE COCKED--SITS MOTIONLESS...WATCHING...SWEATING...

WHAT A BEAST! THE *SIZE* OF IT!

I MUST BUILD A MORE *SUBSTANTIAL* PLACE... AND *QUICKLY!*

T TAKES SHAPE WELL, DOES IT NOT, ALICE?

THANK HEAVENS ARCHITECTURE WAS *NOT* YOUR SELECTED PROFESSION, MY DEAR...

TWO MONTHS LATER...THEIR CABIN IS FINISHED...

NOW...WE CAN WAIT IN SAFETY AND COMFORT... UNTIL WE ARE FOUND!

YES, MY DEAR ...UNTIL... WE ARE...FOUND!

11

19

ONE DAY AS LORD GREYSTOKE WORKS NEAR THE FOREST'S EDGE...

THE MONKEYS ARE FRIGHTENED! I WON—

SUDDENLY-- A FACE... HALF-MAN, HALF BRUTE... JUTS FROM THE DENSE LEAVES!

MY RIFLE... I LEFT IT IN THE CABIN!

IF-IF I CAN ONLY GET PAST—

ALICE...STAY IN THE CABIN! SHUT THE DOOR!

KRACK

ALICE! GO BACK!

UNH...

STRUCK BY THE BULLET, THE APE TURNS IN HEIGHTENED RAGE ON LADY GREYSTOKE...

MORTALLY WOUNDED, THE GREAT BEAST COLLAPSES ON LADY ALICE...

ALICE... ALICE!

HOURS LATER, AS LORD GREYSTOKE WATCHES HIS UNCONSCIOUS WIFE... HER EYES FLUTTER OPEN...

OH, JOHN... IT IS SO *GOOD* TO BE HOME AGAIN...

...IN *ENGLAND!*

YES, YES, MY DEAR... TRY TO SLEEP!

LADY GREYSTOKE NEVER COMPLETELY RECOVERED FROM THAT HORRIBLE EPISODE... EVEN AFTER HER BABY WAS BORN!

SHE NEVER AGAIN STEPPED OUT OF THE CABIN. HER WHOLE LIFE WAS POSSESSED BY HER LITTLE SON AND DEVOTED HUSBAND!

HE'S A FINE BOY, MY DEAR!

WE MUST MAKE PLANS, JOHN... HE WILL ATTEND *ETON*, OF COURSE...

13

21

TWELVE MONTHS PASS....AND THE TINY CABIN EXUDES THE WARMTH OF A HOME....

BUT LORD GREYSTOKE REMAINS EVER ALERT....

THESE TIMBERS WILL KEEP US SAFE....AND THIS **SLIP-LOCK** CANNOT BE OPENED.... BY THE APES!

SEVERAL TIMES, SMALL BANDS OF GREAT APES WOULD VENTURE CLOSE....

A TASTE OF **GUNFIRE** WILL CHANGE THE BEASTS' INTENT!

THEN....ONE YEAR-- **TO THE DAY**--AFTER THE BIRTH OF THEIR SON....LADY ALICE PASSES QUIETLY AWAY....

ALICE....**SOB**....MY DEAREST ALICE!

WHAT....WHAT SHALL WE DO....WITHOUT YOU?

O ALICE, ALICE....WHAT SHALL I DO?

AS LORD GREYSTOKE'S HEAD SINKS IN DESPAIR AND SORROW....A SHORT DISTANCE AWAY, **KERCHAK**, THE KING APE, RAGES WILDLY AMONG HIS TRIBE! HIS PEOPLE TREMBLE....

22

KERCHAK SCREAMS A WILD CHALLENGE TO THE SCATTERED APES.... HIS BARED FANGS GLEAM WICKEDLY FROM FOAMING JAWS....

A LUCKLESS YOUNG MALE COMES TOO CLOSE WITHIN THE ARC OF A VICIOUS SWING.... WITH **FATAL RESULTS!**

THE APE-KING'S RED-RINGED EYES SPY THE SHE-APE **KALA** WITH HER YOUNG BABE.... RETURNING FROM A FORAGE FOR FOOD....

SUDDENLY AWARE OF **KERCHAK'S** TERRIBLE RAGE SHE LEAPS FOR SAFETY....

THE OTHERS WATCH IN STUNNED SILENCE AT THE MACABRE BALLET HIGH IN THE TREETOPS....

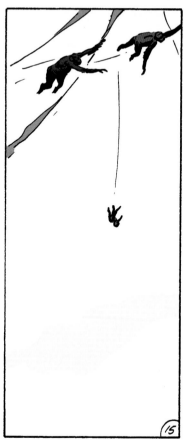

(15)

THOUGHT FOR HER OWN SAFETY IS *GONE*, AS *KALA* SWINGS DOWN TO THE SMALL CRUSHED FORM BELOW...

NOW *KERCHAK'S* TEMPER-RAGE DISAPPEARS AS SUDDENLY AS IT HAD STARTED! CALMLY, HE CALLS HIS TRIBE...

KERCHAK LEADS THEM TOWARDS THE SEA...TO THE STRANGE *WHITE-APE'S* LAIR...

AND *KALA*, TOO, FOLLOWS, STILL CLUTCHING HER DEAD BABY...

WHILE **KERCHAK** AND THE OTHER BULL-APES ATTACK...**KALA** HAS PLACED HER OWN DEAD BABY IN THE MAN-CHILD'S CRADLE... *AND RUNS OFF WITH THE LIVING CHILD!*

LORD GREYSTOKE'S DEFENSE IS BRAVE...BUT **DOOMED!** KERCHAK MOVES FROM THE SLAIN MAN AND APPROACHES THE STRANGE *BLACK-STICK-THAT-ROARS!*

THE KING-APE IS CURIOUS ABOUT THIS STICK THAT HAS HURT AND FRIGHTENED SO MANY OF HIS TRIBE...

17

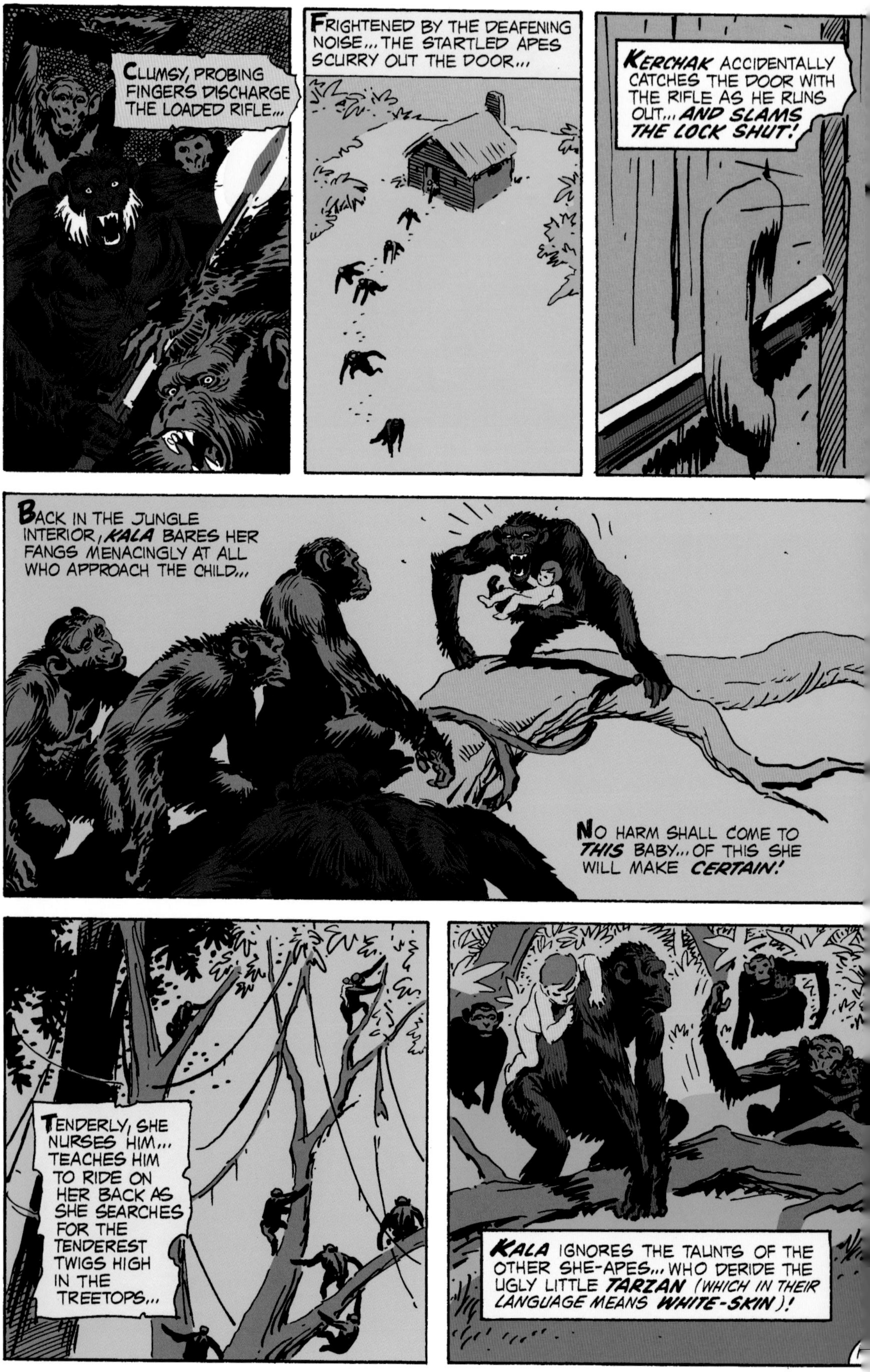
CLUMSY, PROBING FINGERS DISCHARGE THE LOADED RIFLE...
FRIGHTENED BY THE DEAFENING NOISE... THE STARTLED APES SCURRY OUT THE DOOR...
KERCHAK ACCIDENTALLY CATCHES THE DOOR WITH THE RIFLE AS HE RUNS OUT... AND SLAMS THE LOCK SHUT!
BACK IN THE JUNGLE INTERIOR, KALA BARES HER FANGS MENACINGLY AT ALL WHO APPROACH THE CHILD...
NO HARM SHALL COME TO THIS BABY... OF THIS SHE WILL MAKE CERTAIN!
TENDERLY, SHE NURSES HIM... TEACHES HIM TO RIDE ON HER BACK AS SHE SEARCHES FOR THE TENDEREST TWIGS HIGH IN THE TREETOPS...
KALA IGNORES THE TAUNTS OF THE OTHER SHE-APES... WHO DERIDE THE UGLY LITTLE TARZAN (WHICH IN THEIR LANGUAGE MEANS WHITE-SKIN)!

So the son of England's **LORD GREYSTOKE** learns the ways and language of the great apes... having no knowledge of any mother but **KALA** the she-ape!

"See how stupid he is...he will **NEVER** grow! He is weak..."

But none can convince **KALA** to desert the little white ape...

TARZAN'S physical growth is slow compared to his ape brothers who mature in four or five years....

By the age of ten, he has the muscle-power of a man of **THIRTY**!

As he grows, his strength and agility increase... while his mental ability to reason goes beyond that of his ape brothers...

My body is so **UGLY**! Why do I **NOT** have hair...like my handsome brothers? Perhaps....if I rub myself with **MUD**...!

19

27

THE YOUNG *TARZAN* STARES AT HIS REFLECTION IN THE CLEAR WATER...

HOW... *AWFUL* I LOOK! YOU ARE SO FORTUNATE, *KARTUN*...

MY *FACE* LOOKS WORSE THAN MY *BODY!*

SEE HOW *SMALL* MY MOUTH IS... AND SUCH PUNY TEETH!

HARDLY ANY *NOSE* AT ALL... WHILE YOURS IS SO *BROAD* AND *HANDSOME!*

AND—AND MY *EYES!* NOTHING BUT SMALL GREY SPOTS...AND ALL THE REST WHITE!

NOT EVEN *HISTAH*, THE SNAKE, HAS SUCH UGLY EYES!

*R*EACTING INSTANTLY, *TARZAN* DIVES INTO THE COLD WATER... AS *SABOR* THE LIONESS POUNCES...

TARZAN HAS NEVER BEEN IN DEEP WATER BEFORE...AND HIS FIRST LESSON IS *"SINK-OR-SWIM"*!

ATTRACTED BY *TARZAN'S* CALL FOR HELP, THE GREAT APES ARRIVE...

THEY CAN'T UNDERSTAND THIS STRANGE YOUNG WHITE APE... WHO CAN LIE ON *TOP* OF WATER...*AND SMILE!*

WHEN *TARZAN* DISCOVERED THAT HE COULD MAKE A *ROPE* BY TWISTING AND TYING LONG GRASSES... HE MADE LIFE A TORMENT FOR THE ELDERS OF THE TRIBE...

WATCH ME CATCH OLD *TUBLAT*...

ALWAYS, *KALA* IS THERE TO PROTECT HIM...

...FOR--IS SHE NOT HIS *MOTHER?*

TARZAN HAD ALWAYS KNOWN OF THE ODD "NEST" NEAR THE BIG WATER! ONE DAY, WHEN HE IS THIRTEEN YEARS OF AGE...

I WONDER *WHY* THE TRIBE NEVER COMES NEAR THIS PLACE?

THEY WILL NOT EVEN *SPEAK* OF IT!

I NEVER NOTICED *THIS* BEFORE! THE WALL... IT *MOVES*...

KLICK

CREEEEEEAK

*C*AUTIOUSLY...HE ENTERS THE DIM, MUSTY CABIN... *IN WHICH HE WAS BORN!*

IT IS... LIKE THE *NIGHT* IN HERE!

*T*HE THREE SKELETONS (*TWO LARGE, ONE TINY*) HOLD NO INTEREST FOR *TARZAN!* LIFE IN THE JUNGLE HAS ACCUSTOMED HIM TO THE SIGHT OF DEATH IN ITS MANY FORMS...

A
B
C

30

FOR HOURS--UNTIL THE LAST RAY OF SUNLIGHT--HE EXPLORES THE BOOKS AND EXAMINES THE PICTURES...

SOME OF THESE *FLAT PEOPLE...* LOOK... *LIKE ME!*

IT IS *NIGHT...* I MUST *LEAVE!*

WHAT IS *THAT?* SHINING IN THE MOON-LIGHT?

IT IS HARD... AND CUTS LIKE A *SHARP TOOTH!* I WILL TAKE IT WITH ME...

AS HE STEPS FROM THE CABIN, *TARZAN* LOOKS UP TO FIND HIS WAY *BLOCKED...*

...BY THE MENACING FORM OF *BOLGANI,* THE *HUGE BULL-GORILLA* OF ANOTHER TRIBE!

23

31

As he meets the gorilla's charge, *Tarzan* knows he has little chance against *Bolgani*... but the challenge must be met!

Still clutching the hunting knife he found in his father's cabin, *Tarzan* discovers its potent effect as the blade sinks into the beast's flesh...

Bolgani screams in rage and pain... he had expected an *easy* victory...

Bolgani strikes the boy with claw and tusk... as *Tarzan* plunges the long, sharp blade again and again into the blood-matted pelt...

THEN...THE HUGE BEAST TREMBLES... *AND FALLS!* TORN AND BLEEDING, *TARZAN* SLIPS INTO UNCONSCIOUSNESS...

FAR OFF, *KALA* HAS HEARD THE SCREAMS OF BATTLE...AND HER SON IS *NOT* BY HER SIDE! SHE RACES TOWARD THE SOUND...FOLLOWED BY THE REST OF THE TRIBE...

TENDERLY, SHE LIFTS THE BLOODY FORM! MIRACULOUSLY...HE IS *STILL ALIVE!*

THE TRIBE LOOKS ON IN AMAZEMENT AT DEAD *BOLGANI*...SLAIN BY *TARZAN!*

25

GENTLY, THE SHE-APE CARRIES THE LIMP FIGURE BACK TO HER NEST... INTO THE SAFETY OF THE LOFTY TREES...

CAREFULLY SHE LICKS HIS WOUNDS CLEAN...LEAVING FOR SHORT TIMES ONLY TO BRING HIM NOURISHMENT...

TH-THANK YOU, MOTHER...

KLAXTON...*YOU MUST BE OUT OF YOUR MIND!* A BOY...SON OF AN ENGLISH LORD...RAISED BY *APES?*

YOU'VE SEEN HIM *YOURSELF,* MISS...

AND THAT'S ONLY *PART* OF THE STORY!

BUT-- IF IT *IS* TRUE...HE MAY KNOW OF MY FATHER! AND WHERE I CAN FIND HIM--?

BEFORE YE RAISE ANY FALSE HOPES, MISS... LEMME TELL YE THE *REST* OF IT!

NEXT MONTH:
BOOK TWO *OF THE ORIGIN OF*
Tarzan
THE APE MAN!

NEXT ISSUE ON SALE ON OR ABOUT *MAR. 30TH*

34

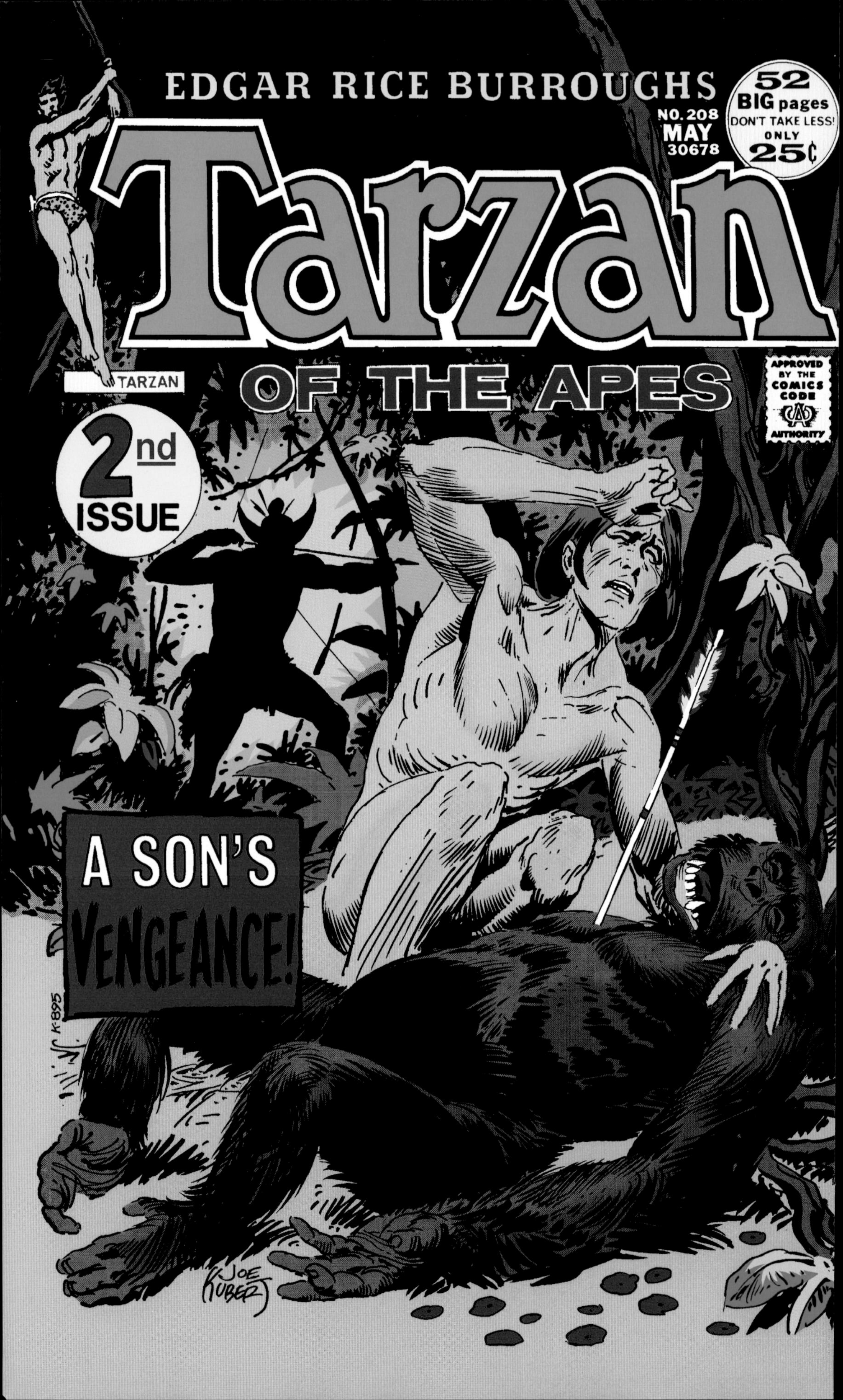
EDGAR RICE BURROUGHS
NO. 208
MAY
30678
52 BIG pages
DON'T TAKE LESS!
ONLY 25¢
TARZAN
OF THE APES
TARZAN
APPROVED BY THE COMICS CODE AUTHORITY
2nd ISSUE
A SON'S VENGEANCE!
JOE KUBERT

A YOUNG GIRL....IN SEARCH OF HER FATHER LOST IN THE TRACKLESS AFRICAN JUNGLE...IS TOLD OF *TARZAN*...THE *MAN* WHO LIVES WITH A TRIBE OF *FEROCIOUS* *APES!*

A SON IS BORN TO THE CAST-AWAYS....AND LADY GREYSTOKE DIES SOON AFTER-WARDS! *KALA,* THE SHE-APE RESCUES THE CHILD....EVEN AS *KERCHAK,* THE APE KING SLAYS THE CHILD'S FATHER!

SHE IS TOLD THAT TARZAN'S PARENTS, *LORD AND LADY GREYSTOKE* HAD BEEN MAROONED IN THE FORSAKEN JUNGLES BY *MUTINEERS...*

AT THE AGE OF THIRTEEN, *TARZAN* (WHOSE NAME MEANS: *WHITE-SKIN*) KILLS *BOLGANI* WITH HIS NEW-FOUND *"IRON TOOTH"!*

JOE KUBER

K-852

KALA, HIS FOSTER APE-MOTHER, CARRIES THE TORN FIGURE TO HER NEST HIGH IN THE TREETOPS....

THERE, SHE TENDS HIM....LICKING HIS WOUNDS CLEAN AND BRINGING HIM NOURISHMENT WHEN HE REGAINS HIS SENSES....

T-THANK YOU.... MOTHER....

AS EVENING CASTS ITS DARK MANTLE OVER THE IMPENETRABLE JUNGLE....AN EERIE, PRIMITIVE RITUAL IS ENACTED! THROUGH FORGOTTEN AGES, INTO A LONG-DEAD PAST....THIS CEREMONY REMAINS *UNCHANGED!* IT IS THE RITE OF THE *DUM-DUM*...AND IN THE MIDST OF THE SAVAGE REVELERS IS *TARZAN* THE APE MAN!

2

IT IS NOT LONG BEFORE *TARZAN'S* SCARS HEAL... AND HIS ROBUST YOUNG BODY IS STRONG AND ACTIVE AGAIN...

THIS IS WHERE I FOUGHT *BOLGANI!*

AHH!

HERE IS THE THING THAT HELPED ME *SLAY* HIM!

MY SMALL, PUNY TEETH SHOW NO *TUSKS*... LIKE MY BROTHERS! BUT-- NOW-- I HAVE A *TOOTH!* LONG... AND *SHARP!*

Tarzan

ORIGIN OF THE APE MAN

A SON'S VENGEANCE

BOOK 2

③

DUM-DUM MARKS IMPORTANT EVENTS FOR THE TRIBE! A VICTORY... THE CAPTURE OR KILLING OF AN ENEMY... THE RECOGNITION OF A NEW KING...

NOW... THE CARCASS OF A SLAIN MARAUDER LAYS INERT BEFORE THE EARTHEN DRUM...

DRIVEN TO A WILD FRENZY, THE TRIBE OF KERCHAK GYRATES AND WHIRLS TO THE MADDENING TEMPO...

ALL VESTIGES OF CIVILIZED MAN ARE GONE... AS TARZAN LEAPS AND SCREAMS IN THE DANCE OF DEATH!

AT THE PEAK OF THE WEIRD RITE, THE CAVORTING FIGURES CONVERGE... THE TIME HAS COME TO DEVOUR THE ENEMY!

WITH HIS KNIFE, TARZAN HAS SEIZED A GENEROUS PORTION... MUCH TO THE DISPLEASURE OF OLD TUBLAT!

THE HATE IN *TUBLAT'S* EYES GIVES WINGS TO *TARZAN'S* FEET...

NIMBLY, THE AGILE LAD TAKES TO THE TREES... PURSUED BY THE SNARLING BEAST!

SCREAM ALL YOU WANT, OLD *DAN-MANGANI!*

THESE BRANCHES WILL NOT HOLD *YOUR* WEIGHT!

*BABOON

ON THE JUNGLE FLOOR BELOW, *KALA* WATCHES THE DRAMA INVOLVING HER SON...

HAVE NO FEAR, MOTHER... HE CAN DO ME NO HARM!

FRUSTRATED, *TUBLAT* TURNS TO VENT HIS TERRIBLE RAGE ON *KALA*...

41

TUBLAT ATTACKS THE SMALLER SHE-APE... HIS FANGS BARED TO SINK INTO KALA'S NECK....

SUDDENLY, A PALE BOLT OF UNLEASHED LIGHTNING DESCENDS FROM THE TREETOPS ONTO TUBLAT'S BACK....

NOW THE TRIBE GATHERS TO WATCH...KNOWING THAT TUBLAT'S PLOY TO LURE TARZAN INTO COMBAT HAS SUCCEEDED....

THE RITUAL OF THE DUM-DUM IS FORGOTTEN...A FIGHT TO THE DEATH IS ABOUT TO BEGIN!

TUBLAT'S PLAN TO ENTRAP *TARZAN* HAS SUCCEEDED *TOO* WELL!

AGAIN AND *AGAIN* THE FLASHING IRON TOOTH STRIKES.... *DEEP AND OFTEN!*

ALL OF *TUBLAT'S* ATTEMPTS TO DISLODGE THE YOUNG FURY....AS THE LOCKED FIGURES ROLL OVER AND OVER....

THE VICTORY CRY OF THE GREAT BULL-APE ISSUES FROM THE THROAT OF THE SON OF AN ENGLISH PEER....*LORD GREYSTOKE!*

COME, *KALA...* NEVER AGAIN WILL *TUBLAT* TROUBLE US!

NOW.... *ALL* KNOW I AM *YOUR SON!*

7

THE NIGHT OF THE *DUM-DUM* IS PAST,... AND A NEW DAY FINDS *TARZAN* APPROACHING THE SMALL CABIN...

ANXIOUSLY, HE RETURNS ONCE MORE TO EXAMINE THE STRANGE MARKS AND PICTURES...

I CANNOT TELL *WHAT* THESE TRACKS ARE.... OR--WHAT ANIMAL HAS MADE THEM?

AHH,... HERE IS A *FLAT THING* THAT LOOKS LIKE.... *ME!* IT HAS NO HAIR ON ITS BODY,... ONLY AN *ODD SKIN* FOR COVER!

UNDER EACH OF *THESE* APES IS THE *SAME TRACKS!* THE SAME MARKS...

RUNNING MAN

PERHAPS,... THESE TRACKS ARE *HOW* THEY MAY BE *RECOGNIZED!* LIKE A *NAME*...

PRIMER 1

HERE IS *NUMA*... AND THE TRACKS ARE *DIFFERENT!*

LION

IT *MUST* BE *NUMA'S* TRACK,... BY WHICH HE IS *KNOWN!*

PRIMER 1

LABORIOUSLY, THE YOUNG *TARZAN* LEARNS TO *READ* A LANGUAGE HE *CANNOT SPEAK!* SLOWLY, HE CONNECTS THE *WORDS* TO THE *PICTURES!*

SPURRED BY A CURIOSITY POSSESSED BY THE YOUNG, HE SNIFFS THROUGH EVERYTHING....

I HAVE NEVER SEEN A STICK LIKE *THIS!* WITH A HARD *BLACK SAP!* IT LEAVES A *MARK* ON MY FINGER....

IT MAKES MARKS ON *OTHER* THINGS! MARKS... LIKE THE NAMES OF THE FLAT THINGS!

THROUGH REPEATED EXPERIMENTS, *TARZAN* TEACHES HIMSELF TO *WRITE*... A LANGUAGE HE *CANNOT SPEAK!*

NOW I KNOW WHY I AM DIFFERENT FROM MY BROTHERS! I AM A *M-A-N!*

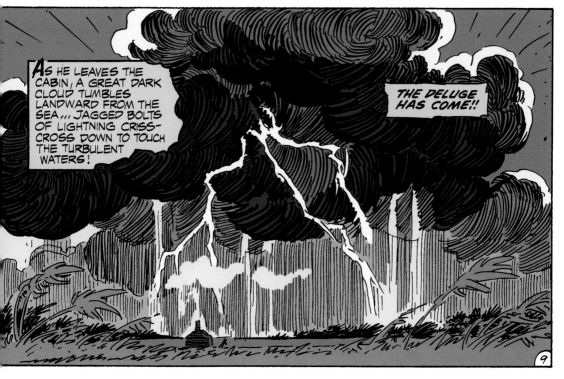

AS HE LEAVES THE CABIN, A GREAT DARK CLOUD TUMBLES LANDWARD FROM THE SEA... JAGGED BOLTS OF LIGHTNING CRISS-CROSS DOWN TO TOUCH THE TURBULENT WATERS!

THE DELUGE HAS COME!!

9

45

THE TROPICAL STORM ERUPTS IN ALL ITS VIOLENCE... AS ROLLS OF THUNDER CRASH AND RAIN POURS DOWN IN SHEETS FROM THE ANGRY SKIES...

NATURE SCREAMS A CHALLENGE TO THE JUNGLE... UPROOTING AND SPLINTERING THE GIANT LEAF-CLAD MONARCHS OF THE FOREST...

AS THE WILD BEASTS SEEK SAFETY FROM ALL THE UNLEASHED FURIES.

TERRIFIED, THE TRIBE OF KERCHAK HOLDS FAST AGAINST THE HOWLING GALE... HOLDING DESPERATELY TO THE BENDING TREES...

46

THE STORM ENDS AS SUDDENLY AS IT HAD BEGUN... AND AMIDST TORN, DRIPPING BRANCHES THE GREAT APES GATHER TO RESUME THEIR LIFE ONCE MORE...

I WOULD NOT SHIVER IF I HAD A *HAIRY SKIN*... LIKE MY BROTHERS...

"...OR--LIKE *SABOR*, THE LIONESS! SHE IS *NEVER* COLD! PERHAPS... I CAN PERSUADE HER TO *GIVE* ME HER WARM COAT!"

WITH HIS NEWLY-BRAIDED ROPE, *TARZAN* WAITS IN CONCEALMENT...

SABOR OFTEN USES THIS PATH ON HER HUNT! I WILL STAY,... TO GREET HER!

YOUR HAIRY SKIN WILL SOON BE *MINE!*

SABOR IS *TRAPPED!* BUT-- ONLY LONG ENOUGH TO TEAR THE GRASS ROPE TO SHREDS....

WITH A ROAR SHE TURNS ON HER TORMENTOR ....WHO STAYS JUST BEYOND REACH OF THE RAZOR-SHARP CLAWS....AND PELTS THE BEAST WITH OVER-RIPE FRUIT!

TARZAN DID NOT ACQUIRE HIS *FUR SKIN*.... BUT HE HAS A BOLD STORY TO TELL HIS *BROTHERS*....

....AND I HAVE MADE A *STRONGER* ROPE! NEXT TIME *SABOR* WILL NOT ESCAPE ME!

AS *TARZAN* ENDS HIS TALE....HE NOTICES *TEEKA'S* ADMIRING GLANCE....

SHE...SHE THINKS I AM BRAVE! AND-- SHE *LIKES* ME!

JUST THEN, *TAUG* (A YOUNG BULL-APE WITH WHOM *TARZAN* HAD PLAYED AS A CHILD) OFFERS TO REMOVE A BOTHERSOME MITE FROM *TEEKA'S* SHINY FUR...

WHY DOES SHE ACCEPT *TAUG'S* ATTENTION...WHEN SHE ADMIRES *ME?*

I WILL CHASE *TAUG* AWAY...

TARZAN ROARS A CHALLENGE...

TAUG ACCEPTS!

AS THE FORMER YOUTHFUL FRIENDS ADVANCE TO DO BATTLE...LITTLE TEEKA DISPLAYS A FEMININE REACTION: EXCITEMENT THAT COMBAT WILL BE FOUGHT FOR HER FAVORS!

13

THE RING OF CHATTERING ANTHROPOIDS SCREAM ADVICE AT THE FIGHTERS... AS A SILKY SHADOW GLIDES SILENTLY OUT OF THE FOREST...

A *HUNGRY* SHADOW...WHO HAS NO INTEREST IN CONTESTS! ONLY IN *FOOD*..

THE SHADOW'S GREEN EYES FASTEN ON THE SLEEK, PLUMP FORM OF *TEEKA*...

TAUG... *TAUG!* LOOK TO TEEKA!

WE MUST HELP *TEEKA*... OR *SHEETA* WILL SLAY HER!

*R*ECOGNIZING A SUPERIOR ADVERSARY, *TAUG* HUSTLES OFF IN THE *OPPOSITE* DIRECTION!

WITH THE SPEED OF **ARA** (LIGHTNING) THE YOUNG MAN-APE RACES AFTER **SHEETA**...

IN ANOTHER MOMENT, THE BLACK FELINE WILL STRETCH HER CLAWS TO GRASP THE HYSTERICAL SHE-APE...

SCREAMING IN FRUSTRATED RAGE, THE GREAT CAT TURNS ON HER CAPTOR WITH UNREASONING FURY...

RUN, SHEETA... **RUN**! TARZAN WAITS FOR YOU!

TRY TO CATCH ME, OLD BAG OF BONES! **I** AM NO FRIGHTENED **SHE**!

15

51

TARZAN PRETENDS TO SLIP AND FALL... AS *SHEETA* LEAPS... EASILY CLEARING THE SPLIT TREE TRUNK....

BUT *TARZAN* HAS SHORTENED THE ROPE...

CHUCKLING TO HIMSELF, *TARZAN* STARTS BACK TO THE TRIBE... HIS GRASS ROPE WILL NOT HOLD THE STRUGGLING CAT FOR LONG!

DANCE, SHEETA-- DANCE!

I WILL TELL *TEEKA* OF YOUR DANCING! SHE WILL LAUGH!

TEEKA IS AGAIN WITH *TAUG*... EVEN THOUGH *HE* RAN AWAY! I-I DO NOT UNDERSTAND THE WAYS OF A SHE!

TURBULENT EMOTIONS CONFUSE HIS MIND... HIS HEART IS HEAVY.... AS YOUNG *TARZAN* APPROACHES THE RUDE, LONELY CABIN IN WHICH HE WAS BORN! AND WHERE HIS PARENTS, *LORD AND LADY GREYSTOKE* DIED!

TARZAN HAS NO KNOWLEDGE OF THE PAST... EXCEPT FOR HIS LIFE WITH THE GREAT APES!

I WILL FILL MY MIND WITH THE *SCRATCHINGS*... AND FORGET *TEEKA!*

IN THESE LEAVES I SEE ALL THE FLAT FIGURES HAVE THEIR *OWN* MATES! JUST AS *TANTOR* THE ELEPHANT HAS HIS... AND *SHEETA* HAS HERS... AND *NUMA* THE LION HAS *HIS!*

I HAVE NEVER SEEN ONE... WHICH STANDS NEAR THIS *M-A-N!*

17

As dusk descends, *TARZAN* leaves the cabin....

*O*NCE MORE IN THE DEEP JUNGLE, HIS SHARP EARS DETECT THE SNAP OF A DRY TWIG! WITHIN SECONDS, HE IS TREE-BORNE....

THAT IS.... A *M-A-N!* LIKE MYSELF! BUT---HE *IS BLACK!* WHILE I AM *WHITE!*

*F*ASCINATED BY HIS FIRST SIGHT OF PEOPLE, *TARZAN* WATCHES FROM HIDING....

THEY ARE MAKING A *BIG NEST...* A PLACE TO LIVE....

*O*PPRESSED AND ENSLAVED BY SOLDIERS, THE NATIVES ARE REFUGEES FROM THEIR OWN LAND....

*D*AWN OF A FATEFUL DAY TEARS A BLOOD-RED SWATH ACROSS THE TROPICAL HEAVENS....

DO NOT HUNT ALONE, *KULONGA!* THIS PLACE IS NEW.... AND DANGEROUS!

AM I NOT YOUR SO *CHIEF M'BONGO* HAVE NO FEAR.... I WILL RETURN WITH FOOD FOR OUR PEOPLE!

A TORRID SUN ARCS HIGH IN THE CLOUDLESS SKY... AS THE SILENT HUNTER SIGHTS AN UNWARY PREY!

KALA, THE SHE-APE, DIGS FOR SOFT ROOTS AND GRUBS.

THE SECOND DEADLY ARROW STRIKES BEFORE THE FULL EFFECT OF THE FIRST IS FELT!

THE POISON-TIPPED BARBS DO THEIR WORK SWIFTLY... AND THE GREAT APE *KALA* LIES LIFELESS ON THE SOFT JUNGLE FLOOR!

THE BEAST'S DYING SCREAMS HAVE ALERTED *OTHERS!*

19

KULONGA DASHES TO THE SAFETY OF THE TALL GRASS....AS THE TRIBE OF KERCHAK APPEARS....

DEEP IN THE INTERIOR, TARZAN HEARS THE DEEP-THROATED CRY OF DISASTER...

KALA?

SWIFTLY HE SCALES THE UPPERMOST BRANCHES AND--LIKE A BIRD--FLIES FROM VINE TO VINE....

MOTHER! WHAT HAPPENED? WHO-WHO DID THIS?

F-FORGIVE ME KALA...I-I SHOULD HAVE BEEN HERE.... TO PROTECT YOU! AS YOU HAVE PROTECTED ME!

A COLD, ICY RAGE GRIPS *TARZAN*... AND IN THE GRUNTING LANGUAGE OF THE GREAT APES HE ASKS A QUESTION...

WHERE IS THE ONE WHO DID THIS?

"A HAIRLESS APE... *GOMANGANI!* HE RAN ON TWO LEGS... *THERE!*"

❋ BLACK APE!

WITH THE UNERRING SENSE OF A JUNGLE BEAST, *TARZAN* FOLLOWS THE TRAIL VISIBLE ONLY TO HIS KEEN EYES...

SOON...

THERE HE IS... A M-A-N... LIKE MYSELF!

HE STANDS BEFORE *HORTA* BRAVELY!

HE HAS SLAIN *HORTA*... WITH THE LITTLE POINTED STICK... AS HE DID *KALA!*

THAT STICK MUST HAVE A *SECRET POWER!*

21

As *KULONGA* TURNS TO BUTCHER HIS KILL.... A NAKED FIGURE HURTLES DOWN FROM THE TREES....

THE BLACK WARRIOR LASHES OUT AT THE WILD THING...

KALA'S DEATH IS AVENGED... BUT *TARZAN* FEELS NO ELATION!

*S*TRIPPING THE DEAD MAN OF HIS GARMENT, *TARZAN* HOISTS THE BODY ONTO HIS SHOULDER...

THE SKIN HE WORE WILL BE MINE.... AND HIS BRAVERY IN BATTLE WILL BE FOREVER PART OF *ME!*

SOFT VELVET NIGHT CLOAKS THE SILENT MOVEMENT NEAR THE VILLAGE PERIMETER....

HIS TRIBE WILL FIND HIM HERE!

HIGH IN THE TREETOPS ONCE MORE, *TARZAN* SCANS THE COMPOUND...

THE "SHE" PUTS *DEATH* ON THE POINTED STICKS!

AHHH.... THEY HAVE DISCOVERED THEIR LOST BROTHER!

*D*ROPPING LIGHTLY TO THE NEAR-DESERTED VILLAGE....

I WILL HAVE USE FOR THESE....

TARZAN KNOWS HE HAS BUT SECONDS BEFORE THE PEOPLE RETURN...BUT HIS ATTENTION IS CAUGHT BY THE CONTENTS OF A NEARBY HUT...

WHO CAN TELL WHAT IMPULSE CAUSED THE BOY TO PLAY THIS BIT OF MISCHIEF...? TO CREATE THIS REARRANGEMENT?

BUT...THUS BEGINS THE LONG LEGEND SURROUNDING THE AWESOME POWERS OF *TARZAN* LORD OF THE JUNGLE!

23

59

A FUNERAL PROCESSION BEARING *KULONGA'S* BODY IS DISRUPTED BY THE DISCOVERY OF *TARZAN'S* TABLEAU...

*P*LEASED WITH THE REACTION, *TARZAN* MELTS INTO THE DENSE JUNGLE UNDERGROWTH...

*I*N THE DAYS THAT FOLLOW, THE APE-MAN PRACTICES WITH BOW AND ARROW... AND ACHIEVES GREAT PROFICIENCY!

NOW I WILL MEET *SABOR,* THE LIONESS... AND ONLY *ONE* OF US WILL EVER HUNT AGAIN!

60

IT IS A GOOD TIME TO HUNT...

A *SIXTH-SENSE* WARNS THE MAN-BEAST THAT...IN THE JUNGLE...THE *HUNTER* CAN BECOME THE *HUNTED!*

INSTANTLY, THE POISON-LADEN BARB FLIES INTO THE BREAST OF THE ATTACKING LIONESS...

THE GREAT CAT IS DEAD BEFORE HER BODY FALLS TO THE JUNGLE FLOOR...AND *TARZAN* VENTS THE BLOOD-CURDLING VICTORY SCREAM OF THE *BULL-APE!*

25

61

LATER...*TARZAN* DISPLAYS THE SLAIN LIONESS' PELT TO THE TRIBE OF *KERCHAK!*

SEE WHAT *TARZAN*, THE MIGHTY HUNTER, HAS DONE? WHO ELSE AMONG YOU HAS DEFEATED ONE OF *NUMA'S* PEOPLE?

PERPLEXED, THE JUNGLE MAN STOPS...THE APE'S LANGUAGE HAS *NO* WORD FOR *MAN!* AND *TARZAN* HAS NEVER LEARNED TO *SPEAK* AS A *MAN*...

TARZAN IS MIGHTY! *TARZAN* IS NO APE...*TARZAN* IS—

THE APE TRIBE REJOICES THE CONQUEST OF THEIR ENEMY, *SABOR!*...ALL, EXCEPT THE KING APE, *KERCHAK!* JEALOUSY AND HATRED GLEAM FROM HIS SMALL EYES!

CAN SUCH A PERSON ACTUALLY *EXIST*, KLAXTON? AND-- COULD HE HELP ME FIND MY FATHER?

WHO KNOWS, MA'AM? ANYWAYS...WE'D HAVE T'*FIND* THE WILD MAN FIRST!

BUT...THE *WILD MAN* DOESN'T HAVE TO BE FOUND! HE *NEVER LEFT*...

NEXT MONTH:
BOOK THREE: ORIGIN OF
Tarzan
THE APE MAN!

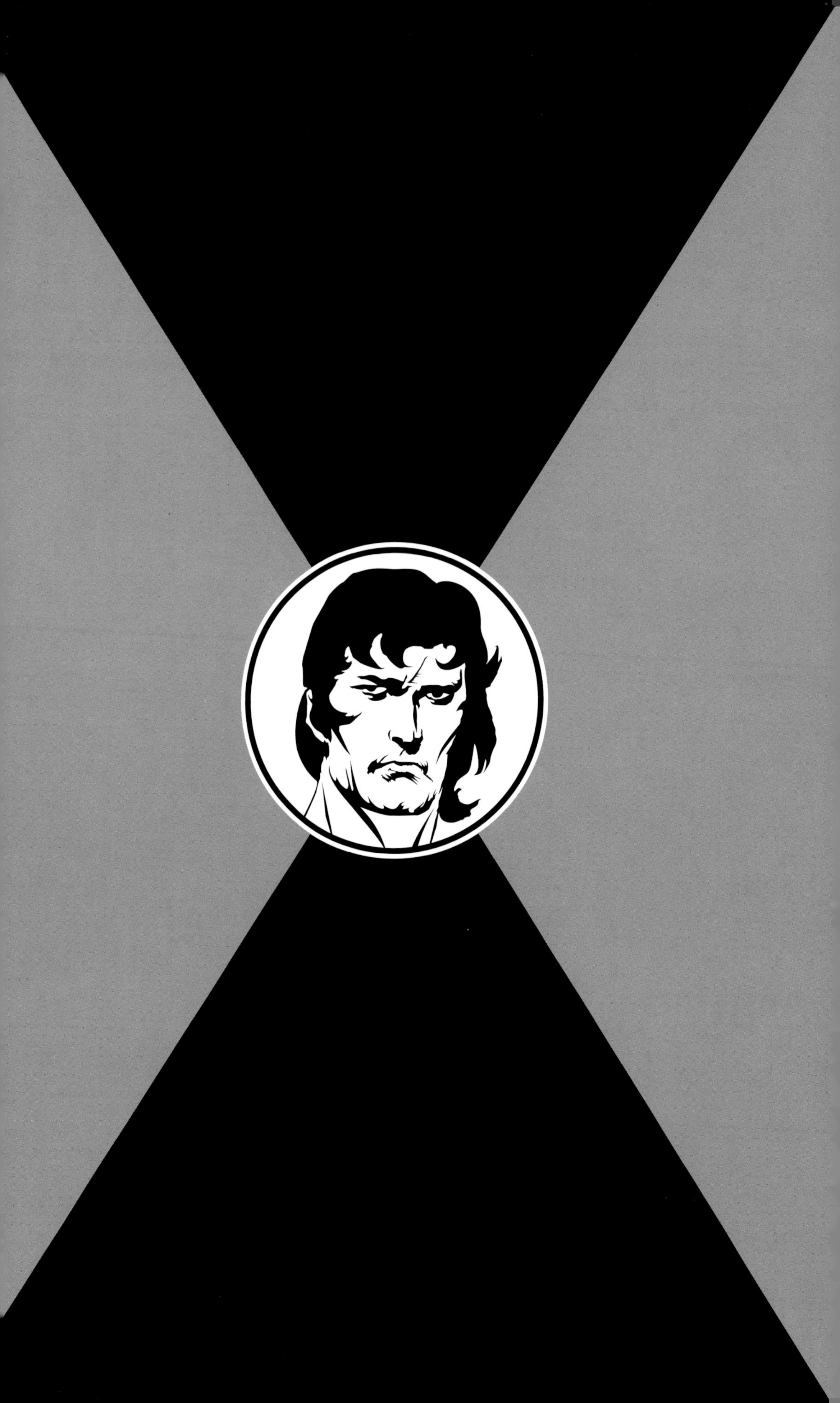

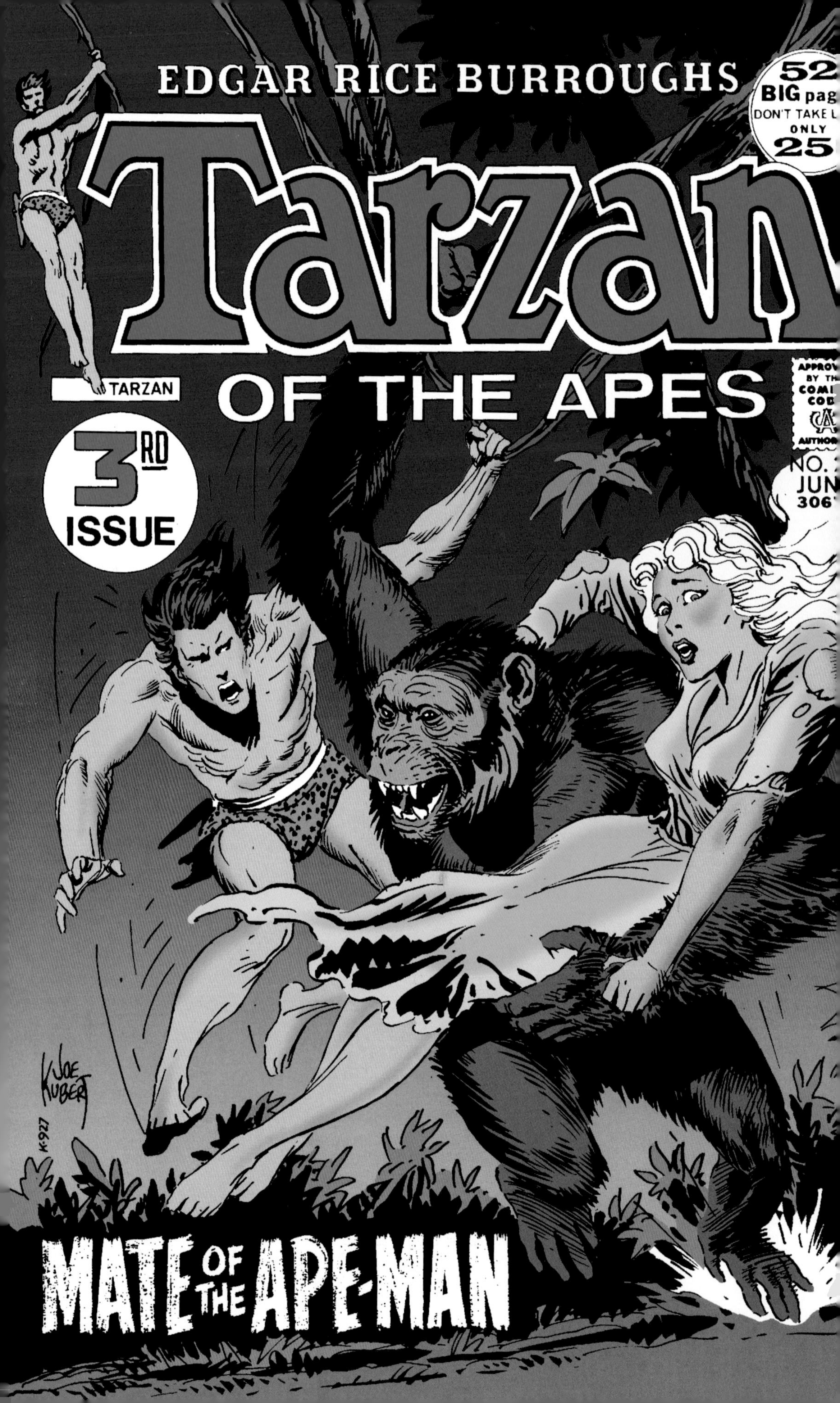
EDGAR RICE BURROUGHS
TARZAN
OF THE APES
TARZAN
3RD ISSUE
52 BIG pag
DON'T TAKE L
ONLY
25
NO.
JUN
306
JOE KUBERT
MATE OF THE APE-MAN

DEEP IN THE STEAMY, IMPENETRABLE AFRICAN JUNGLE, *TWO WILD FIGURES* SCREAM A CHALLENGE... THAT MUST BE ANSWERED BY THE LOSER'S *DEATH!*

THE ARENA IS FORMED BY A CIRCLE OF *GIANT APES (THE TRIBE OF KERCHAK)*...WHO CHATTER AND GRUNT IN EXCITED ANTICIPATION....

K-897

"NOW, *TARZAN*-- YOU WILL FEEL THE FANGS OF *KERCHAK!*"

A SHUDDERING TREMOR....AND **KERCHAK** IS DEAD!

I AM **TARZAN**... KING OF THE APES!

THAT'S... **INCREDIBLE,** KLAXTON! AN **APE-MAN**... RAISED IN THE JUNGLES?

IT'S LIKE I TOL' YE, MA'AM! THE BLINKIN' NATIVES THINK HE'S A **DEVIL**...AN'...WHO'S T'SAY HE **AIN'T?**

WIELDING HIS KNIFE WITH DREADFUL EFFECT, *TARZAN* IS UNAWARE THAT IT WAS *KERCHAK* WHO HAD MURDERED HIS FATHER *(LORD GREYSTOKE)* MANY YEARS AGO...

EDGAR RICE BURROUGHS
Tarzan

ORIGIN OF THE APE-MAN

A MATE FOR THE APE-MAN

BOOK 3

AND WITH LORD GREYSTOKE'S OWN BLADE, THE BOY METES OUT JUSTICE TO THE CRUEL *KERCHAK*...

DEVIL OR ANGEL... HE MAY BE THE ONE TO HELP ME *FIND MY FATHER!*

AYE...IF HE'S A *MIND* TO, THAT IS!

BUT--LEMME TELL YE THE REST OF IT-- LIKE I HEARD IT TOL' T' *ME!*

MAYBE...AFTER YE'VE HEARD IT *ALL*... YE WON'T BE SO ANXIOUS FER HIS HELP!

SO...LET US CONTINUE THE STRANGE STORY OF *TARZAN OF THE APES!*

3

KALA...TARZAN'S FOSTER APE-MOTHER ...HAS BEEN SLAIN BY *KULONGA*, SON OF A NATIVE CHIEF....

HIS YOUNG HEART BURSTING WITH GRIEF, *TARZAN* EXACTS HIS VENGEANCE....

THE YOUNG APE-MAN TEACHES HIMSELF TO USE THE DEAD MAN'S BOW AND ARROW... AND WITH IT DISPATCHES THE APE-TRIBE'S WORST NEMESIS-- *SABOR, THE LIONESS!*

NOW...HAVING CONQUERED *KERCHAK*, THE KING APE...*TARZAN* (SON OF AN ENGLISH LORD) STAND AS UNDISPUTED LEADER OF THE APES!

"*TARZAN IS A GREAT HUNTER TARZAN IS MIGHTY... TARZAN IS KING!*"

LATER... ALONE IN HIS CABIN...

I CANNOT READ *THESE* TRACKS...AS I HAVE THE *OTHER* BUNCHES OF LEAVES! BUT-- I WILL SAVE IT,...AND *THIS*!

IRONICALLY, *TARZAN'S* MOST PRIZED OBJECTS FOUND IN THE CABIN ARE HIS *MOTHER'S LOCKET*...HIS *FATHER'S DIARY* (WRITTEN IN FRENCH)... AND A PHOTOGRAPH OF HIS FATHER!

I WILL TELL THE TRIBE...NO LONGER WILL I LEAD THEM! *TARZAN* IS NOT AN APE! *TARZAN* IS A *M-A-N*!

As *TARZAN* DROPS LIGHTLY TO THE GROUND...

T IS *TERKOZ*! BEATING AN OLD SHE!

AT *TARZAN'S* ORDER TO STOP, *TERKOZ* TURNS IN RAGE...HIS LIPS FOAMING... TUSKS BARED!

5

69

HEAD LOWERED, THRUSTING FORWARD FROM HIS BULL-MUSCLED NECK, *TERKOZ* GRUNTS A CHALLENGE...

"*DOES THE MIGHTY TARZAN FEAR TERKOZ... THAT HE NEEDS HIS LONG TOOTH TO DO BATTLE?*"

TO BEAT *TERKOZ... TARZAN* NEEDS ONLY HIS *BARE HANDS!*

COME, FIGHTER OF OLD SHES... KILLER OF TOADS...

I HAVE NO LONG TOOTH!

*E*MITTING THE REVERBERATING ROAR OF THE GREAT BULL-APE, *TERKOZ* HURTLES AT THE APE-MAN...

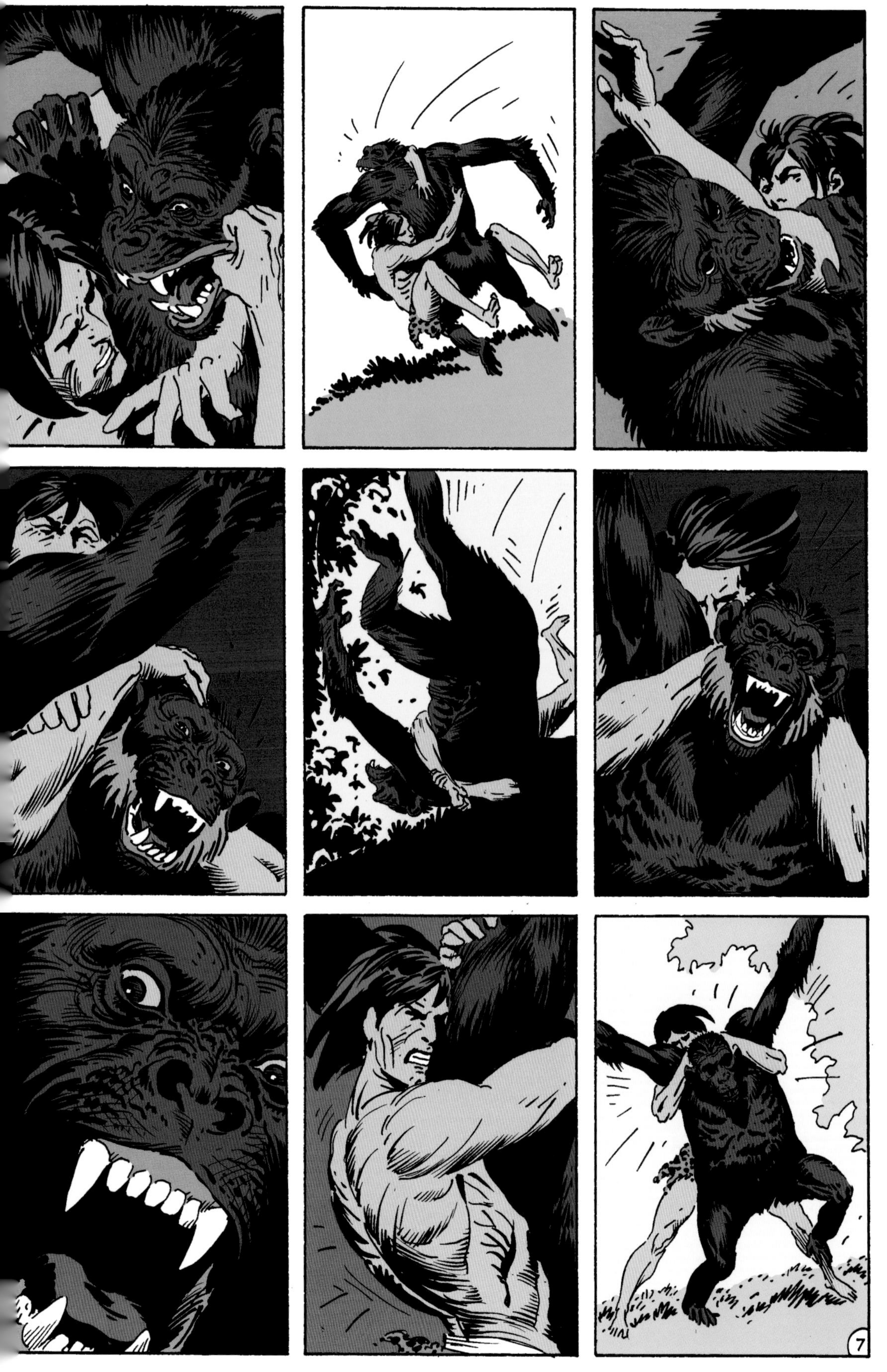
7

REALIZING THAT THE DEATH OF *TERKOZ* WOULD SERVE NO PURPOSE... *TARZAN* DEMANDS HIS SURRENDER!

KA-GODA?

*"KA-GODA!"

* SURRENDER

TERKOZ IS BANISHED FROM THE TRIBE! HE WILL LIVE BY HIM- SELF... IN THE JUNGLE!

AND.... *TARZAN*, TOO, MUST LEAVE.... TO FIND HIS OWN PEOPLE! FAREWELL....

STRUCK DUMB BY THEIR KING'S ABDICATION, THE APES STARE SILENTLY AS *TARZAN* LEAPS LIGHTLY INTO THE TREES....

THROUGH THE DAYS THAT FOLLOW, STORIES COME BACK TO THE NATIVE VILLAGE.... OF THE *GIANT WHITE APE* THAT FEW HAVE SEEN.... AND NONE HAVE LIVED TO TELL ABOUT!

IN HIS CABIN...

I WILL CUT... THE *HAIRS*... FROM MY FACE!

TARZAN IS *NO APE!* HE IS A *M-A-N*... LIKE THE FLAT THINGS IN THE BOUND BUNCH OF LEAVES!

ONE MORNING, UPON RETURNING FROM A HUNT,.... *TARZAN* SIGHTS AN UNUSUAL SPECTACLE....

M-A-N...WHITE... LIKE MYSELF! THEY COME FROM MY CABIN .... TOWARDS THEIR OWN!

THEIR HOME.... *FLOATS ON THE GREAT WATER!*

HEAVE TO, YE *BILGE RATS!* GIT BACK T' THE SHIP!

RIGHT Y'ARE, CAP'N,... THEN-- WE GITS RID O' THEM PASSENGERS --AN' SPLIT TH' *TREASURE!*

SHET YER FACE, SNIPE! OR *NOTHIN'* IS WHAT YOU'LL GIT!

LOOKIT, CAP'N .... *BEHIND YER!*

ONLY THING *YOU'LL* BE GITTIN', CAP'N, IS A *BULLET* TWIXT YER SHOULDER BLADES!

C'MON, MEN... THE TREASURE'S **OURS**, NOW! AN' ONE **LESS** T' SPLIT WITH!

RIGHT Y'ARE, **SNIPE!**

THESE **M-A-N** THINGS ARE NO DIFFERENT THAN THE **GOMANGANI!..** NO WISER THAN THE **APES**...NO LESS CRUEL THAN **SABOR!**

SWIFTLY, THE APE-MAN SPEEDS TO THE CABIN...

THEY HAVE SCURRIED THROUGH HERE LIKE **MANU** THE MONKEY!

THEY DID NOT FIND **MY** TREASURE!

IF THEY HAD... THEY WOULD FEEL THE WRATH OF **TARZAN!**

HUNH! THEY RETURN... WITH OTHERS!

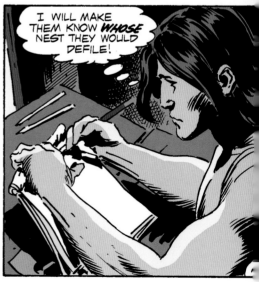

I WILL MAKE THEM KNOW **WHOSE** NEST THEY WOULD DEFILE!

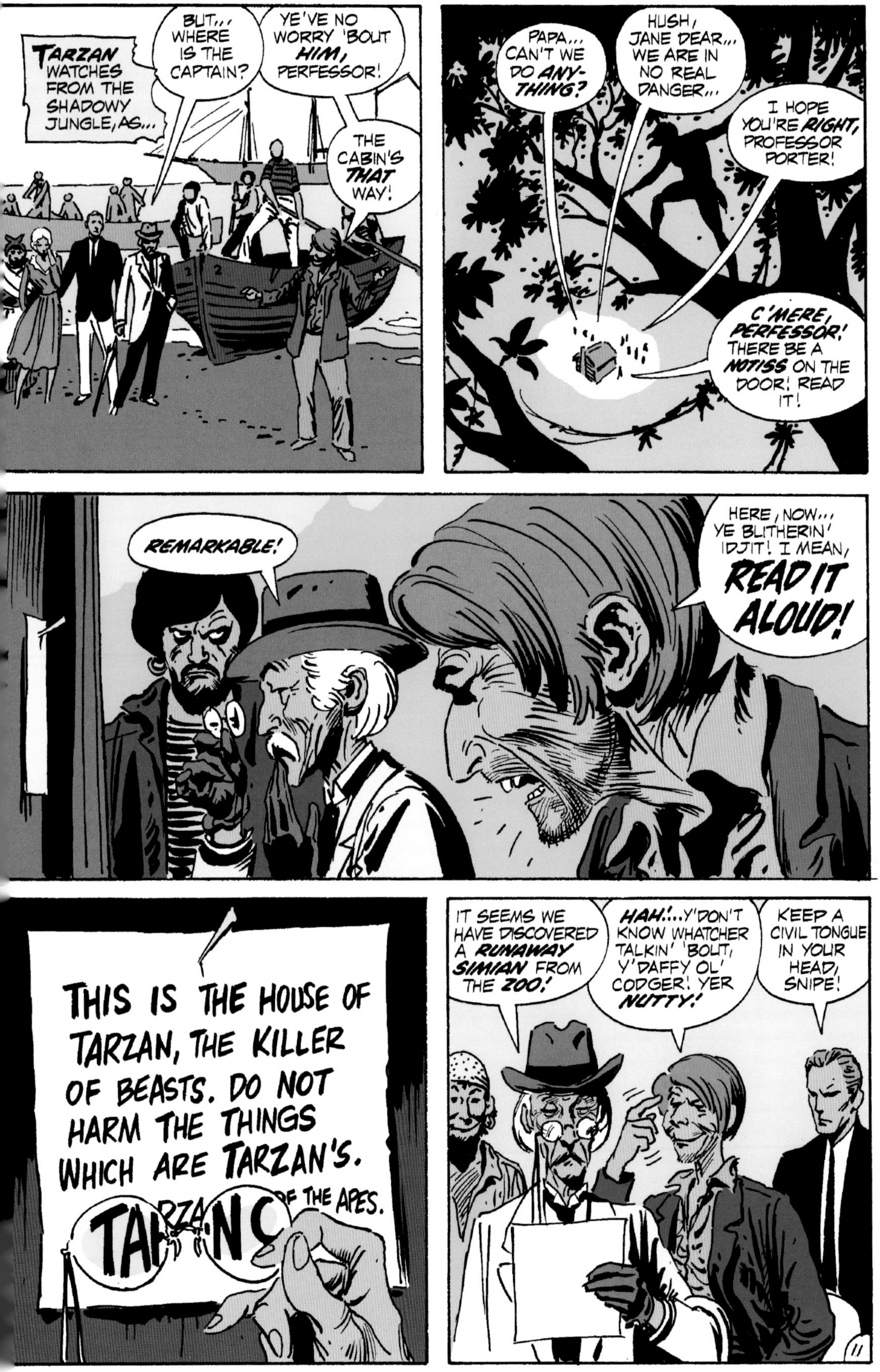
TARZAN WATCHES FROM THE SHADOWY JUNGLE, AS...
BUT... WHERE IS THE CAPTAIN?
YE'VE NO WORRY 'BOUT HIM, PERFESSOR!
THE CABIN'S THAT WAY!
PAPA... CAN'T WE DO ANYTHING?
HUSH, JANE DEAR... WE ARE IN NO REAL DANGER...
I HOPE YOU'RE RIGHT, PROFESSOR PORTER!
C'MERE, PERFESSOR! THERE BE A NOTISS ON THE DOOR! READ IT!
REMARKABLE!
HERE, NOW... YE BLITHERIN' IDJIT! I MEAN, READ IT ALOUD!
THIS IS THE HOUSE OF TARZAN, THE KILLER OF BEASTS. DO NOT HARM THE THINGS WHICH ARE TARZAN'S.
OF THE APES.
IT SEEMS WE HAVE DISCOVERED A RUNAWAY SIMIAN FROM THE ZOO!
HAH!...Y'DON'T KNOW WHATCHER TALKIN' 'BOUT, Y'DAFFY OL' CODGER! YER NUTTY!
KEEP A CIVIL TONGUE IN YOUR HEAD, SNIPE!
11

EH? HOW'S THAT? MR. WILLIAM CLAYTON WANTS TO BE A *HERO*, DOES HE?

YOU'VE MURDERED THE CAPTAIN... AND *ROBBED* US!

EVEN WITH A GUN--YOU'D NEVER SHOOT A MAN... *EXCEPT IN THE BACK!*

HIDDEN IN THE HEAVY JUNGLE UNDERGROWTH... *TARZAN* CANNOT UNDERSTAND THE ANGRY WORDS... BUT HE RECOGNIZES A COWARD'S ACT!

SNEER AT *ME*, EH, MR. BRITISH NOBILITY? *THIS'LL* TAKE TH' STARCH OUTER YER BACK!

AT THAT MOMENT, THREE THINGS HAPPEN SIMULTANEOUSLY: JANE PORTER SCREAMS... A SLIM SPEAR PIERCES SNIPE'S SHOULDER... AND HIS GUN DISCHARGES HARMLESSLY INTO THE GROUND!

IN THE CONFUSION THAT FOLLOWS, YOUNG CLAYTON RECOVERS THE WOUNDED MAN'S GUN...

WHO-WHO THREW THAT SPEAR, WILLIAM?

WHOEVER HE IS, I THANK HIM!

HSST... HIDE THIS GUN, MISS PORTER!

FATHER... *FATHER!* OH, ESMERALDA... WHERE DID HE GO?

BOTH OF YOU STAY INSIDE THE CABIN... I'LL FIND YOUR FATHER!

Minutes later...

THE CREWMEN...HAVE TAKEN *SNIPE* BACK TO THE SHIP, ESSIE! WE'D BEST STAY IN HERE...

YES, MISS JANE! B-BUT...SEE HERE WHAT'S INSIDE THIS PLACE?

L-LOOKS LIKE... WE AIN'T *REALLY* ALL ALONE... MISS JANE!

WE-WE *MUST* STAY HERE... INSIDE...AND WAIT!

WILLIAM WILL SOON RETURN... W-WITH FATHER! WE....*MUST WAIT!*

13

77

MEANWHILE, THE COWARDLY CREW HASTILY PULLS OFF FROM THE BEACH...

GIT BACK TO TH' SHIP!

WE'VE GOT TH' TREASURE! LEAVE THE BLIGHTERS T ROT HERE!

ARROW

UNKNOWN TO WILLIAM CLAYTON, HE IS BEING WATCHED BY NONE OTHER THAN HIS OWN COUSIN...SON OF HIS LOST UNCLE, JOHN CLAYTON (LORD GREYSTOKE)...

PROFESSOR... PROFESSOR PORTER! WHERE ARE YOU?

HUNH! THAT ONE CRIES OUT IN A STRANGE TONGUE!

NUMA HAS HEARD HIM, AS WELL!

DOES THE M-A-N NOT KNOW OF NUMA'S ARRIVAL?

SUDDENLY...THE SHRILL, HORRIBLE CRY OF THE BULL-APE SHATTERS THE JUNGLE QUIET...

WH-WHAT WAS THAT?

A SUN-BRONZED FIGURE HURTLES ONTO *NUMA'S* BACK....

THERE IN THE TWILIGHT DEPTHS OF THE AFRICAN JUNGLE, YOUNG CLAYTON WATCHES A SCENE THAT MIGHT HAVE TAKEN PLACE IN SOME PRIMORDIAL TIME AT THE DAWN OF MAN...

I-I CAN'T BELIEVE MY EYES! *A MAN...* FIGHTING A *WILD LION!*

THE ACT IS ACCOMPLISHED SO QUICKLY...THAT BEFORE CLAYTON CAN EVEN MOVE--

THAT SCREAM... THE SAME AS I HEARD BEFORE!

15

TH-THANK YOU... MR.-ER... WHATEVER-YOUR-NAME-IS!

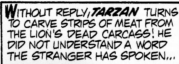

WITHOUT REPLY, TARZAN TURNS TO CARVE STRIPS OF MEAT FROM THE LION'S DEAD CARCASS! HE DID NOT UNDERSTAND A WORD THE STRANGER HAS SPOKEN...

N-NO, THANK YOU,...I'LL--PASS UP THIS MEAL!

HE'S,... MOTIONING FOR ME TO FOLLOW! I GUESS,... I'VE NO CHOICE!

SUDDENLY--THE DISTANT SOUND OF A GUNSHOT REVERBERATES THROUGH THE JUNGLE...

JANE... IT'S JANE!

BACK IN THE CABIN, THE TWO WOMEN SAT HUDDLED IN THE GROWING DARKNESS...

M-MISS JANE,...I HEARS SOMETHIN'!... SCRATCHIN'!... OUTSIDE!

SLOWLY, *SABOR* INSINUATES HER GREAT BODY THROUGH THE LATTICE-GRILLED WINDOW...

...AS JANE FIRES THE SMALL PISTOL... *AND MISSES!*

IT'S *JANE!* WE'VE GOT TO GET BACK TO THE CABIN,... SHE'S IN *TROUBLE,* I KNOW!

TARZAN SENSES CLAYTON'S MEANING... AND MOTIONS FOR HIM TO GRASP HOLD!

*F*OLLOWING *TARZAN'S* MIMED INSTRUCTIONS, CLAYTON TAKES HOLD OF THE APE-MAN, AND...

HE PICKS HIS WAY THROUGH THESE DARKENED TREES,... AS I WOULD STROLL A *LONDON STREET* AT HIGH NOON!

*T*HE NEXT FEW MINUTES WOULD NEVER BE FORGOTTEN BY THE CULTURED ENGLISH LORD! FROM ONE BRANCH TO ANOTHER,... HUNDREDS OF DIZZYING FEET ABOVE THE JUNGLE FLOOR,... SPEEDS THE APE-MAN!

17

I—I CAN'T DECIDE... WHETHER HE'S MORE *BEAST* THAN *MAN!*

HE CARRIES ME AS IF I WERE... A *BABY!*

WITHOUT WARNING *TARZAN* DESCENDS TO THE GROUND...

WE'RE AT THE CABIN! *LOOK*... THE WINDOW!

TARZAN SHRUGS OFF HIS PASSENGER AND RACES TO THE CABIN...

INSIDE THE CABIN...

HELP... OH, HELP US... SOMEONE!

COME, SABOR... TARZAN WISHES TO PLAY WITH YOU!

In the flick of an eye-lash, *Tarzan* leaps...

WILLIAM,,, DID *YOU*--?

NO, MY DEAR,,,,NOT I! THE BRAVE MAN WHO SAVED YOU,,,, IS ALREADY *GONE!*

Hours later, professor porter returns to the small cabin,,,,

PAPA,,,, YOU'VE COME BACK!

YES, YES, JANE,,,, AT THE INSISTENCE OF A *WILD MAN!*

PROFESSOR,,, WAS HE WEARING A *LEOPARD SKIN*?

WHY,,, *YES,,,*

INCIDENTALLY, MR, CLAYTON,,, I ALSO SAW OUR SHIP! *HEADING OUT TO SEA!*

THAT CUT-THROAT CREW HAS *LEFT* US HERE,,,, *FOR-EVER!*

THE NEXT DAY...

PROFESSOR,...I AM *CERTAIN* THAT THOSE SKELETONS ARE THE LAST REMAINS OF *LORD AND LADY GREYSTOKE*... AND THEY MUST BE BURIED PROPERLY!

YES, OF COURSE...

NOT FAR AWAY... *TARZAN* WATCHES!

THESE PEOPLE ARE STRANGE! THEY MAKE A RITUAL OF BURYING *OLD BONES!*

FROM HIS PERCH, THE APE-MAN SCANS THE SHORE, AND...

THE *OTHERS* HAVE RETURNED!

WHAT IS THAT,... FAR OUT ON THE WATER? *SMOKE...*

IT'S A GOOD THING WE GOT BACK HERE IN TIME,... T'BURY TH' TREASURE!

YER *RIGHT,* SNIPE! THAT *FRENCH CRUISER* WAS ON OUR TAIL!

WELL,...HURRY UP AN' *BURY* IT! WHATCHER WAITIN' FER?

SNIPE,...I'M SICK O' YER ACTIN' LIKE A BLOODY *BOSS...*

CHEW ON *THIS,* SNIPE!

AFTER BURYING THE CHEST IN THE SOFT SAND *(ALONG WITH SNIPE'S BODY!)*...

BACK TO TH' SHIP, BOYS...WE'LL GIT TH' TREASURE AT A SAFER TIME!

THAT *FRENCH CRUISER'S* COMIN' CLOSER...

TARZAN MUSES... AS HE WATCHES...

M-A-N IS MORE FOOLISH--MORE *CRUEL*--THAN ANY BEAST IN THE JUNGLE!

SPURRED BY CURIOSITY, *TARZAN* QUICKLY UNCOVERS THE CHEST...

THEY MUST *VALUE* THIS BOX! THEY WISH TO KEEP IT *SAFE*!

I WILL KEEP IT *FOR* THEM...

FOUR SAILORS HAD SWEATED UNDER THE BURDEN THAT *TARZAN* SO LIGHTLY TOSSES ONTO HIS BROAD SHOULDERS...

...DEEP IN THE FOREST... WHERE *NO ONE* BUT *TARZAN* WILL KNOW!

THAT NIGHT...

THE SHE WRITES...UNDER A LIGHT, LIKE THE ✳ *SUN!* AND--HER HAIR IS LIKE GOLDEN STRANDS SPUN BY THE JUNGLE SPIDERS! SHE IS...BEAUTIFUL...

✳ LAMP

AFTER THE CABIN IS DARK,...AND ALL ARE ASLEEP...

21

HIGH IN THE TREETOPS,...AS DAWN'S FIRST LIGHT STREAKS THE HEAVENS...

THESE TRACKS,... ARE *NOT* LIKE THE ONES I KNOW! YET,...THEY *ARE* ALIKE,...IN SOME WAYS! I MUST STUDY THIS...

IT IS NOT LONG BEFORE *TARZAN* IS ABLE TO DECIPHER JANE'S *HANDWRITING*... AND HE READS THE LETTER JANE HAS WRITTEN TO A FRIEND, DESCRIBING ALL THAT HAD TRANSPIRED...

I AM TARZAN OF THE APES. YOU ARE JANE PORTER, I SAW IT IN YOUR LETTER. I AM YOURS, YOU ARE MINE. LIVE WITH ME, TOGETHER, IN MY HOUSE, FOREVER. I LOVE YOU.

AS *TARZAN* APPROACHES THE CABIN,...TO DELIVER HIS NOTE...

EVERYONE,... IS *GONE!* WHERE--?

A SCREAM!

IT IS... JANE!

A SHORT WHILE BEFORE, TERKOZ HAD COME UPON JANE AND ESMERALDA IN THE FOREST...

TERKOZ SEIZED THE GIRL AND TOOK TO THE TREES WHILE JANE SCREAMED IN TERROR.

THOSE SCREAMS WERE HEARD BY *TARZAN!*

86

DIRECTED BY AN ANIMAL SIXTH-SENSE, *TARZAN* SOON CATCHES SIGHT OF THE FLEEING EXILE AND HIS PRIZE! THE APE-MAN'S HEART THRUMS WITH ANTICIPATION OF THE BATTLE TO COME...

YOU CANNOT ESCAPE ME, *TERKOZ!* EVEN *HISTA,* THE SNAKE, HAS MORE COURAGE THAN *YOU!*

"TERKOZ AWAITS TARZAN!" AND WHEN YOU ARE SLAIN, I WILL *KEEP* YOUR MATE... AND RETURN AS *KING OF THE TRIBE."*

LIKE TWO CHARGING BULLS THEY MEET...LONG CANINES OF THE APE PITTED AGAINST THE MAN'S THIN-BLADE!

23

IN MINGLED HORROR AND FASCINATION, JANE WATCHES THE TITANIC STRUGGLE... WHOSE OUTCOME WILL DECIDE *HER FATE!*

MOMENTS LATER, THE *LIFE-OR-DEATH* CONTEST IS DECIDED....

LIFTING HIS WOMAN IN HIS ARMS, *TARZAN* CARRIES JANE INTO THE JUNGLE...

AND... IS THAT... *ALL?*

HARDLY, MA'AM! THE STORY WHAT FOLLOWS... IS EVEN *STRANGER* THAN WHAT'S ALREADY HAPPENED!

NEXT MONTH: BOOK 4
THE ORIGIN OF
Tarzan OF THE *APES!*

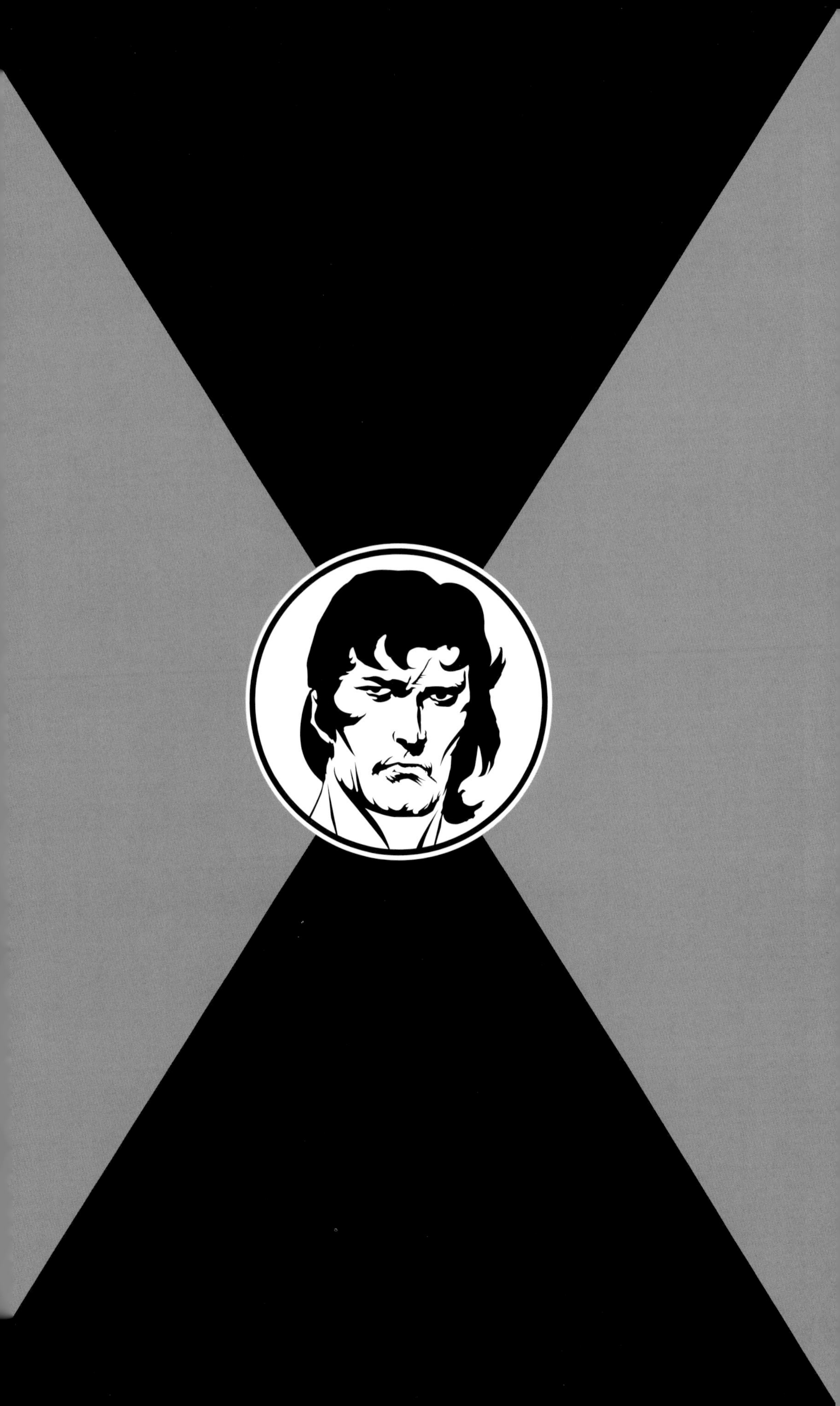

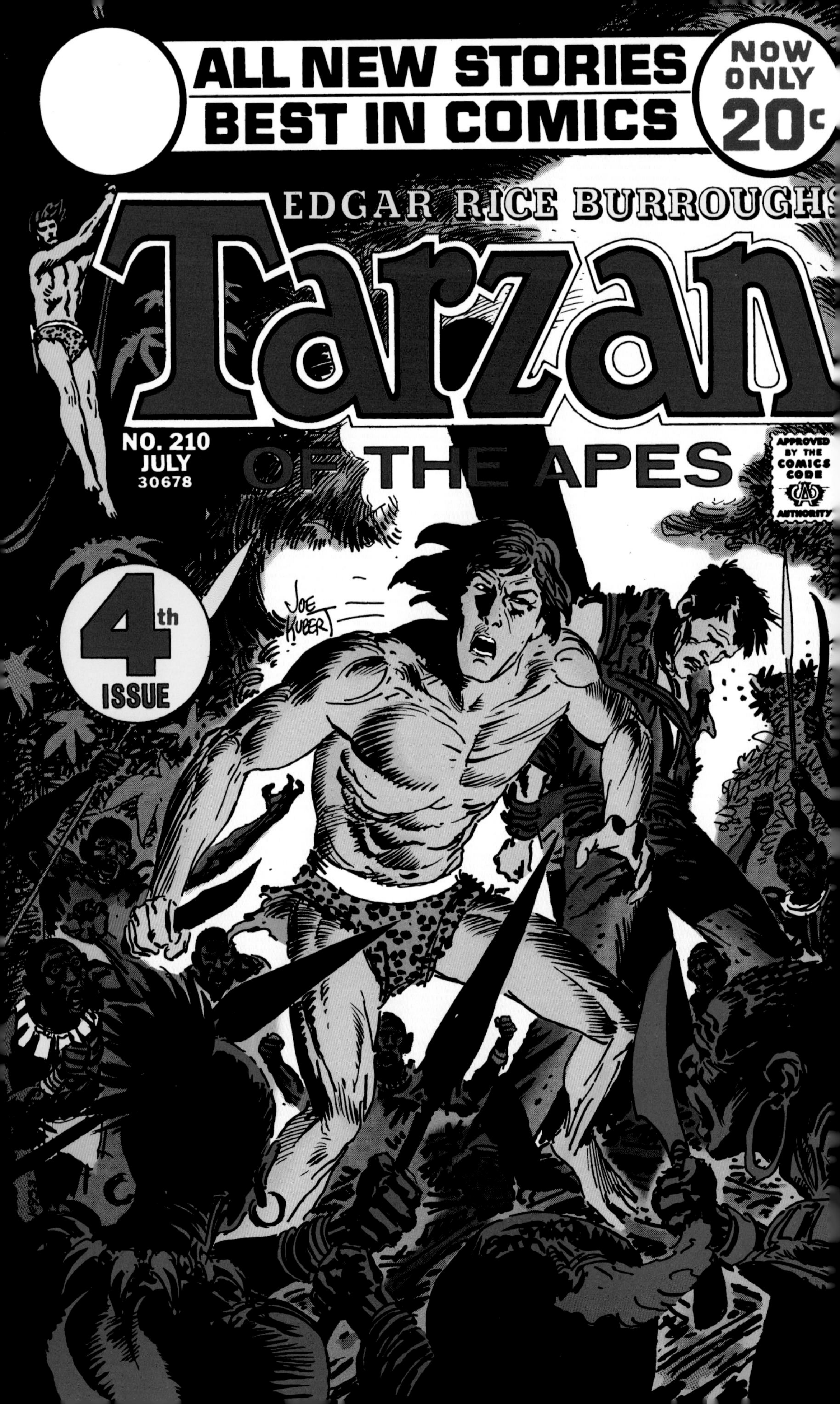

ALL NEW STORIES
BEST IN COMICS
NOW ONLY 20¢
EDGAR RICE BURROUGHS
Tarzan
OF THE APES
NO. 210
JULY
30678
APPROVED BY THE COMICS CODE AUTHORITY
4th ISSUE
JOE KUBERT

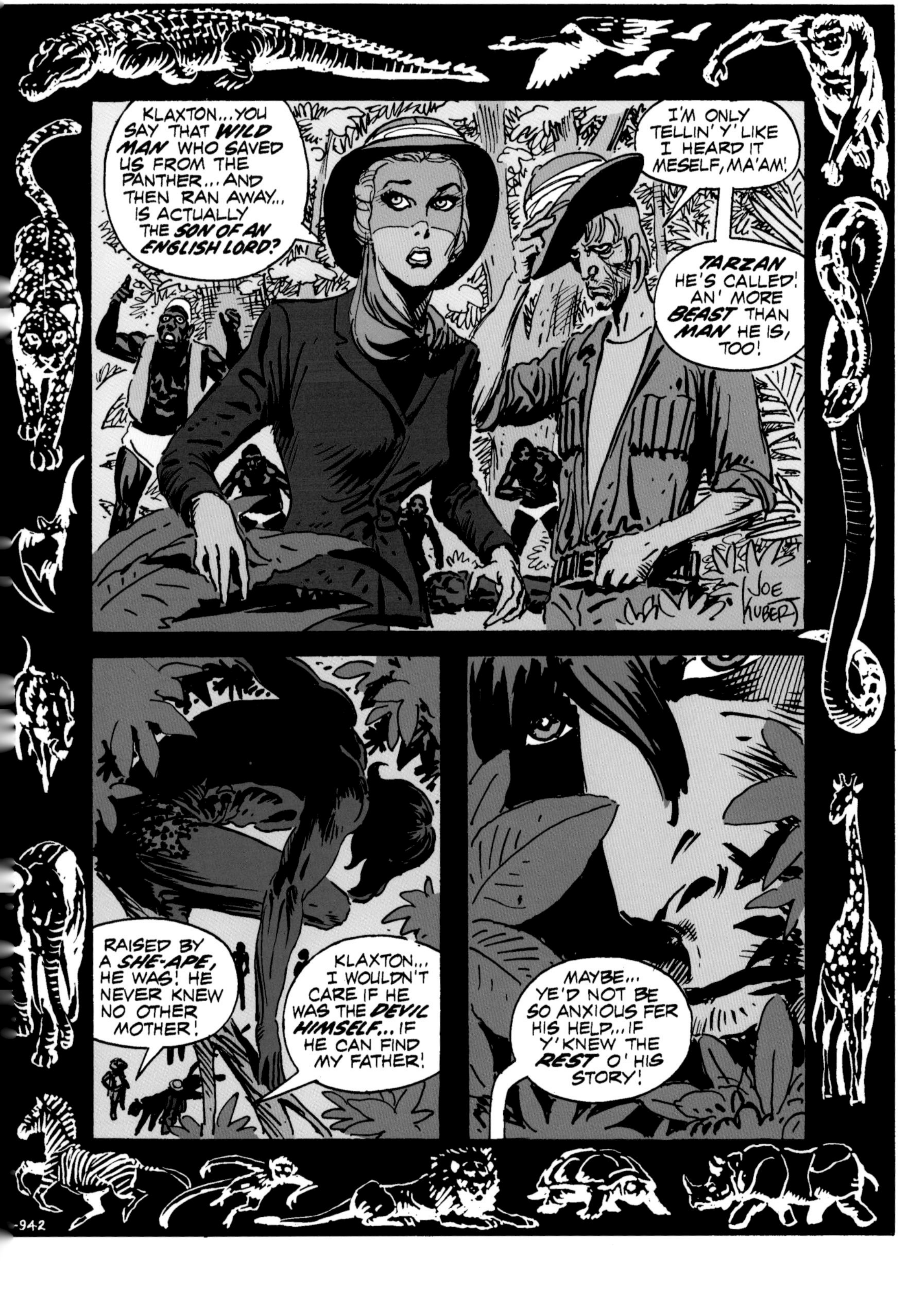
KLAXTON... YOU SAY THAT WILD MAN WHO SAVED US FROM THE PANTHER... AND THEN RAN AWAY... IS ACTUALLY THE SON OF AN ENGLISH LORD?
I'M ONLY TELLIN' Y' LIKE I HEARD IT MESELF, MA'AM!
TARZAN HE'S CALLED! AN' MORE BEAST THAN MAN HE IS, TOO!
JOE KUBERT
RAISED BY A SHE-APE, HE WAS! HE NEVER KNEW NO OTHER MOTHER!
KLAXTON... I WOULDN'T CARE IF HE WAS THE DEVIL HIMSELF... IF HE CAN FIND MY FATHER!
MAYBE... YE'D NOT BE SO ANXIOUS FER HIS HELP... IF Y'KNEW THE REST O' HIS STORY!
-942

AND SO FOLLOWS THE INCREDIBLE TALE AS HEARD BY THE WHITE-HUNTER... WHISPERED IN HUSHED, FRIGHTENED TONES BY THOSE WHO *KNOW*...OF A *MAN*-- RAISED BY THE GREAT APES--TO BE THEIR *KING!*

TARZAN'S ENTIRE EXISTENCE CHANGES WHEN *JANE PORTER* AND HER COMPANY ARE STRANDED IN AFRICA...AND SHE IS KIDNAPPED BY *TERKOZ*, RENEGADE BULL-APE!

*B*ORNE THROUGH THE HIGHEST JUNGLE TREES, JANE FEELS NO FEAR! ONLY A *THRILL* TO THE STRONG ARMS ABOUT HER...AND THE LOOK OF AFFECTION FROM THE CLEAR, GREY EYES SET IN THAT NOBLE FACE!

THE *JUNGLE LORD'S* PURSUIT IS UNFLAGGING...

HIS JUSTICE IS *SWIFT*... AND *CERTAIN!*

AND THE LOVE BETWEEN A MAN AND WOMAN DISPELLS ALL BARRIERS OF TIME AND SPACE...

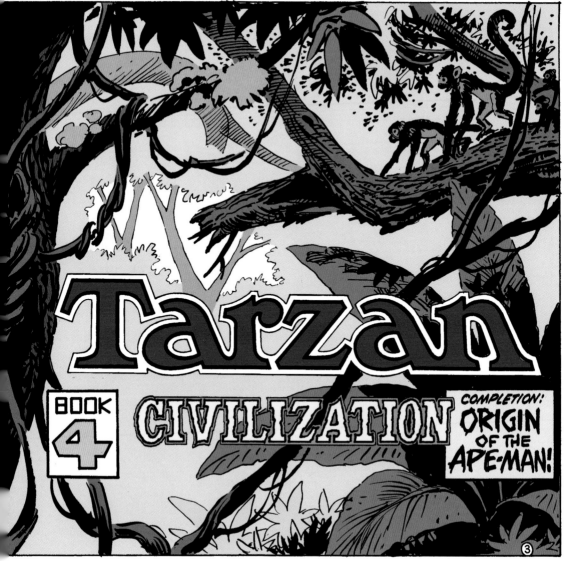

Tarzan

BOOK 4 CIVILIZATION

COMPLETION: ORIGIN OF THE APE-MAN!

③

AT THE CABIN *WILLIAM CLAYTON* READIES A SIGNAL FIRE PYRE...

M-MR. CLAYTON... *MR. CLAYTON...*

WHAT IS IT, ESSIE...?

WHERE IS MISS PORTER?

SHE-SHE BEEN TAKEN BY... *A APE!*

OH (SOB) LAWDY...

WE-WE WAS WALKIN' IN THE WOODS... WHEN THIS (SOB) *WILD THING* COME JUMPIN' DOWN... AN' *TOOK HER!*

OHH... WHAT WE GOIN' TO *DO,* MR. CLAYTON?

P-POOR MISS JANE...

WE-WE'VE *GOT* TO GET HER BACK... SOMEHOW...

MR. CLAYTON... LOOK! OVER THERE...

IT'S... A *SHIP,* ESMERALDA!

A *FRENCH CRUISER*...WITH THE *ARROW* IN TOW!

IN MINUTES, ROARING FLAMES ATTRACT THE CRUISER'S LOOKOUT...

THEY SEE US, ESMERALDA... *THEY SEE US!*

94

THANK HEAVENS YOU SAW OUR SMOKE...

WE NEED YOUR HELP... DESPERATELY!

I AM LT. D'ARNOT OF THE FRENCH NAVY...

AT YOUR SERVICE, M'SIEUR!

WE HAVE LEARNED OF YOUR DILEMMA... FROM THE SURVIVORS OF THE SHIP ARROW!

ALLOW ME TO EXPLAIN...

"FOR MANY DAYS WE HAVE PURSUED THE ARROW... AND SHE WOULD NOT ANSWER OUR CALLS FOR RECOGNITION!"

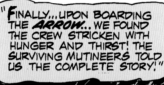

"FINALLY... UPON BOARDING THE ARROW... WE FOUND THE CREW STRICKEN WITH HUNGER AND THIRST! THE SURVIVING MUTINEERS TOLD US THE COMPLETE STORY!"

LT. D'ARNOT... A GIRL IS LOST... IN THAT GREEN HELL!

SLOWLY, M'SIEUR... TELL ME ALL YOU KNOW!

BREATHLESSLY, THE TERRIBLE STORY TUMBLES FROM CLAYTON'S LIPS... AND MINUTES LATER...

ALONS, MON BRAVES!

WE MUST FIND THE POOR GIRL BEFORE... IT IS TOO LATE!

In the deepest recesses of the vast jungle....*Jane Porter* waits for the return of *Tarzan!* Her heartbeats quicken as he approaches...bearing food! For, though she cannot understand *why*... she knows she *loves* this wild man of the forest...

I DO SO WISH YOU COULD SPEAK...THERE IS SO MUCH I WOULD LIKE TO KNOW ABOUT YOU!

WHERE DID YOU COME FROM? WHERE ARE YOUR PEOPLE? HOW--?

Tarzan CAN ONLY SPEAK HIS APE LANGUAGE, WHICH SOUNDS LIKE A CHATTERING GIBBERISH TO JANE...

WHAT IS THIS LOCKET?

TARZAN PLACES HIS LOCKET AROUND JANE'S NECK...

NOW...YOU MUST TAKE ME BACK TO MY FATHER! HE...WILL BE TERRIBLY WORRIED...

*I*NTUITIVELY, THE *JUNGLE LORD* UNDER-STANDS THE REQUEST...

...*A*ND HOURS LATER, AS THE RED SUN SETS ON A VERDANTLY LUSH HORIZON...

TARZAN DROPS TO THE GROUND NEAR THE CABIN...

IN THE RAPIDLY-DARKENING JUNGLE, *LT. D'ARNOT* LEADS THE SEARCH PARTY...WHEN, *SUDDENLY*...

...*T*HE SHADOWS COME TO LIFE...AND HE IS SEIZED BY A *DOZEN ARMS!*

7

A SHORT DISTANCE BEHIND...CLAYTON AND *D'ARNOT'S* MEN ARE MET BY A LETHAL VOLLEY OF SPEARS AND ARROWS...

GET BACK! THOSE SPEARS ARE *POISONED!*

THEY HAVE TAKEN LT. D'AR—

UNH!

IT'S TOO DARK...TO SEE *ANYTHING!*

MAKE CAMP...BACK IN THE CLEARING WE PASSED! WE...MUST WAIT...UNTIL *DAYLIGHT!*

THE TRIBE OF *M'BONGA* HAS BEEN PERSECUTED AND DRIVEN BY THE WHITE INVADERS OF THEIR CONTINENT! NOW...THEY WILL EXACT *REVENGE*...ON THEIR CAPTIVE!

THE SAVAGE *DANCE OF DEATH* HAS BEGUN... AND D'ARNOT SAGS HEAVILY, AS HIS PAIN-WRACKED BODY TWITCHES AT EVERY CUT AND BLOW!

WHY... DO I -- NOT *DIE?* RELEASE ME... FROM THIS... PAIN...

SUDDENLY, ONE OF THE TAUNTING HORDE GASPS... DROPS HIS WEAPON... CLAWS CONVULSIVELY AT HIS THROAT...

...AND, SECONDS LATER, FALLS TO EARTH WITH A SICKENING THUD!

9

IT-IT IS *MUNANGO KEEWATI*...THE EVIL ONE OF THE JUNGLE!

FROM HIGH IN THE TREES THERE ISSUES FORTH THE WILD ROAR OF THE *GREAT BULL-APE!*

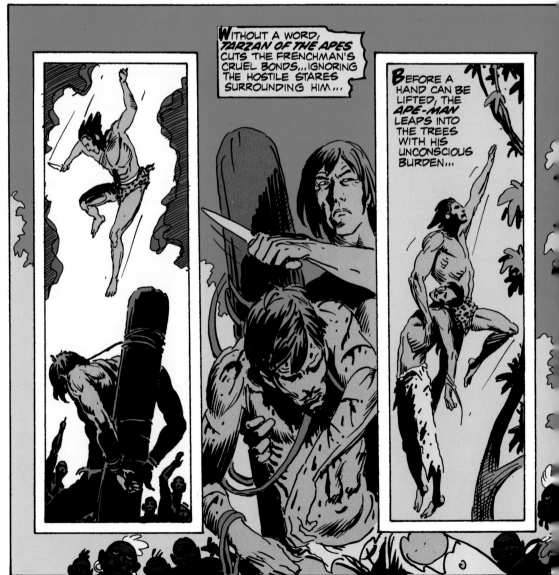

WITHOUT A WORD, *TARZAN OF THE APES* CUTS THE FRENCHMAN'S CRUEL BONDS...IGNORING THE HOSTILE STARES SURROUNDING HIM...

BEFORE A HAND CAN BE LIFTED, THE *APE-MAN* LEAPS INTO THE TREES WITH HIS UNCONSCIOUS BURDEN...

EARLY NEXT MORNING, THE SEARCH PARTY LIMPS INTO THE CABIN CLEARING... BEARING THE BODIES OF THEIR DEAD AND WOUNDED COMRADES...

JANE... JANE PORTER!

IS--IS IT REALLY *YOU?*

THANK GOD YOU ARE SAFE! WE FEARED THE WORST... WHEN ESMERALDA TOLD US OF THE *GORILLA!*

I-I'M QUITE ALL RIGHT, WILLIAM... THE *FOREST MAN* RESCUED ME!

PANGS OF JEALOUSY TWIST CLAYTON'S HEART...

OH...? SO-- THAT *HALF-SAVAGE* SAVED YOU, EH?

AND... WHERE IS HE NOW?

HE... RETURNED INTO THE JUNGLE...

HMMM... POSSIBLY TO JOIN HIS TRIBE...

...THE *SAME TRIBE* THAT ATTACKED US... *KILLED* OUR MEN... AND CAPTURED *LT. D'ARNOT!*

T'S... *NOT TRUE!* I... WILL *NEVER* BELIEVE THAT! HOW CAN YOU ACCUSE A MAN WHO SAVED *YOUR* LIFE... OF SUCH DREADFUL ACTS?

HE... WILL COME BACK! HE WILL *PROVE* YOU ARE *WRONG!*

POSSIBLY, MISS PORTER! BUT-- ANYONE CAN TELL YOU HE IS ONLY A *BEAST OF THE JUNGLE!*

AS HE STRIDES AWAY FROM JANE'S HURT GLANCE, CLAYTON'S MIND GOES BACK...

PROFESSOR... *PROFESSOR!* ANSWER ME...

HOW COULD I BE SUCH A *CAD?* TO MAKE INSINUATIONS... ABOUT A MAN WHO CAME TO MY AID...?

"I HAD NO IDEA ANYONE WAS WATCHING ME... FROM BEHIND THE HEAVY FOLIAGE..."

"*T*HE DAY WE WERE PUT ASHORE ON THIS STRANGE LAND! WHEN I SEARCHED FOR PROF. PORTER...IN THE JUNGLE..."

IT-IT'S GROWING DARK! I *MUST* RETURN TO THE CABIN... BEFORE...I'M COMPLETELY *LOST!*

WHA-? IT'S... A *LION!* HE'S AFTER *ME!*...NOWHERE TO RUN--

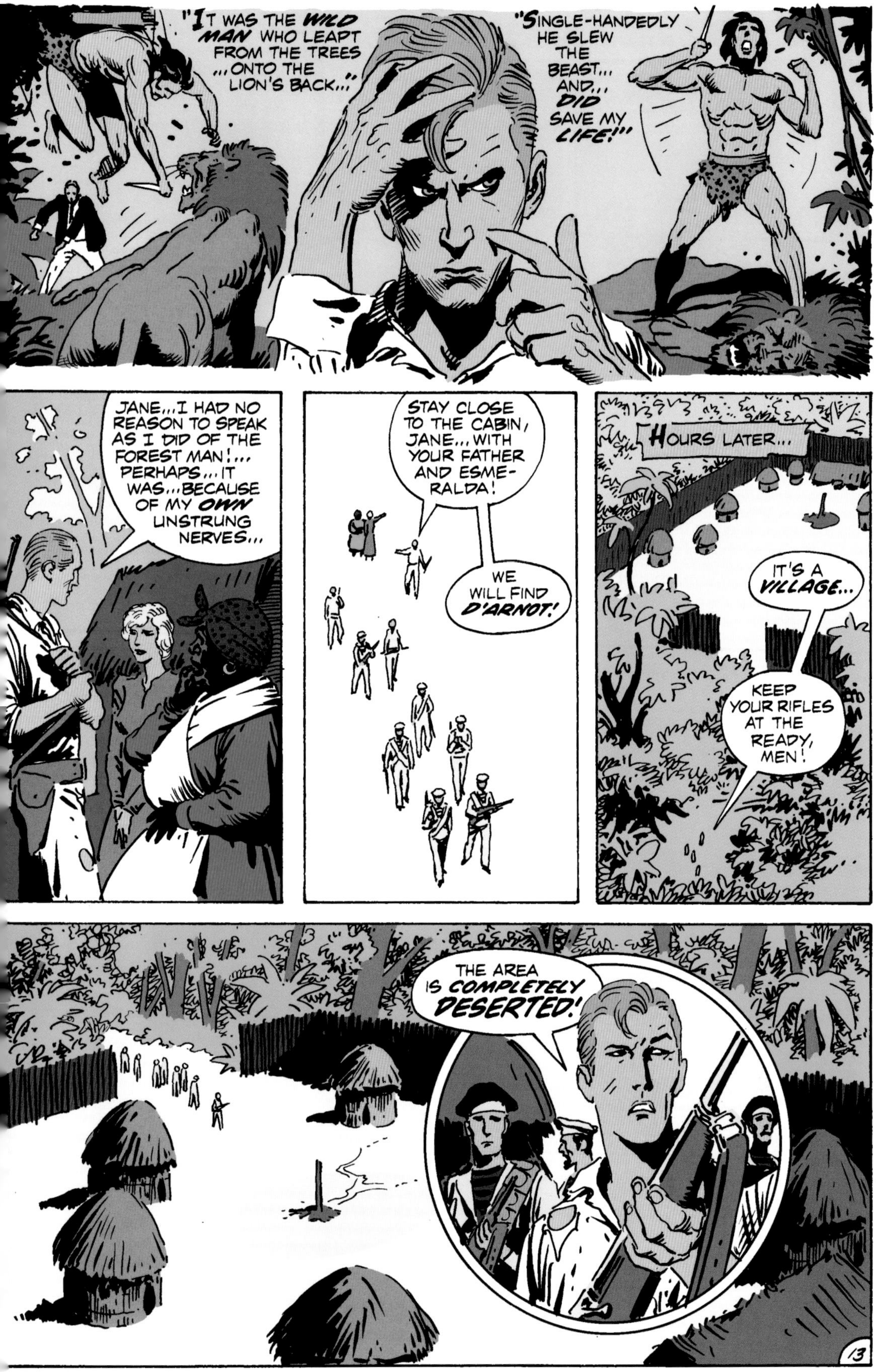
"IT WAS THE WILD MAN WHO LEAPT FROM THE TREES ...ONTO THE LION'S BACK..."
"SINGLE-HANDEDLY HE SLEW THE BEAST... AND... DID SAVE MY LIFE!"
JANE... I HAD NO REASON TO SPEAK AS I DID OF THE FOREST MAN!... PERHAPS... IT WAS... BECAUSE OF MY OWN UNSTRUNG NERVES...
STAY CLOSE TO THE CABIN, JANE... WITH YOUR FATHER AND ESME-RALDA!
WE WILL FIND D'ARNOT!
HOURS LATER...
IT'S A VILLAGE...
KEEP YOUR RIFLES AT THE READY, MEN!
THE AREA IS COMPLETELY DESERTED!
13

DRIVEN BY A SUPERSTITIOUS FEAR OF *MUNANGO KEE-WATI*...THE NATIVES HAVE FLED THEIR COMPOUND...

M'SIEUR CLAYTON... *LOOK HERE!* IN THESE ASHES...

WHAT IS IT?

A SHRED OF *LT. D'ARNOT'S* UNIFORM...WITH *BLOOD* ON IT!

I FEAR HE IS... *NO MORE!*

SOME DISTANCE AWAY... HIGH IN THE JUNGLE'S TALLEST TREE...

WH-WHERE AM I?...WHO-?

UNH...NOW I REMEMBER! YOU--SAVED ME--FROM THE SAVAGES!

D'ARNOT WATCHES IN AMAZEMENT AS THE WILD CREATURE WRITES ON A SMOOTH PIECE OF TREE-BARK...

I AM TARZAN OF THE APES. WHO ARE YOU?

DURING THE DAYS IT TAKES D'ARNOT TO RECOVER HIS STRENGTH, HE TEACHES *TARZAN* TO SPEAK FRENCH ...AND THE APE-MAN IS AN APT PUPIL!

TARZAN EXPLAINS HOW HE RESCUED JANE FROM THE RENEGADE *TERKOZ* D'ARNOT IS ASTOUNDED...

TARZAN TELLS D'ARNOT OF HIS EARLY LIFE AMONG THE GREAT APES... WHEN HE BECAME THEIR KING... AFTER SLAYING KERCHAK!

"MUNGO WISHES TO STEAL MY SHE..."

"THAKA IS TOO OLD..."

ONE DAY, YOU TOO WILL BE OLD, MUNGO!

LEAVE THAKA AND HIS SHE IN PEACE,... OR YOU WILL ANSWER TO ME!

TARZAN DESCRIBES HIS NOCTURNAL VISITS TO THE NATIVE VILLAGE... BENT ON OBTAINING FOOD AND IMPLANTING FEAR IN THE HEARTS OF THE SUPERSTITIOUS PEOPLE!

SOON, THE SUPERSTITIOUS NATIVES SET ASIDE FOODSTUFFS FOR "MUNANGO-KEEWATI"; THE EVIL SPIRIT OF THE JUNGLE,...

I MUST LEAVE THE APES,...AND FIND MY OWN PEOPLE...

NOW THAT YOU ARE WELL, D'ARNOT... WE WILL RETURN TO THE CABIN! I WILL CARRY YOU...

I AM TOO HEAVY, MON AMI... IT IS TOO FAR—

WITH A LOW CHUCKLE, THE APE-MAN LIFTS D'ARNOT LIKE A BABE... AND GLIDES SWIFTLY THROUGH THE TREES!

YOU CONSTANTLY AMAZE ME, TARZAN... ALREADY, WE ARE HERE!

BUT-- MY SHIP! IT IS... GONE!

EVERYONE HAS GONE! THEY LEFT A RIFLE... AMMUNITION... FOOD!

THEY MUST INTEND TO RETURN...

...BUT-- WHEN?

SHE DID NOT WAIT...

SEE HERE, TARZAN... THERE IS A LETTER! FOR YOU!

TARZA

TARZAN-?

FAR TO THE EAST, *TARZAN* HURTLES THROUGH THE TERRACED TREE-SCAPE,... EVEN AS *TANTOR,* THE ELEPHANT, SHRIEKS A GREETING, THE APE-MAN DOES NOT ACKNOWLEDGE...

THE JUNGLE-MAN PRESSES FORWARD...OBLIVIOUS TO ALL ABOUT HIM,...IN A FUTILE ATTEMPT TO ESCAPE *HIS OWN THOUGHTS!*

SHE DID NOT WAIT,... FOR ME!

ALONE IN THE CABIN, AS NIGHT FALLS...

HOW WILL I EXIST HERE.... *ALONE?*

WILL THE SHIP RETURN...BEFORE THE *BEASTS* OR THE *SAVAGES* FIND ME?

WH-WHAT'S THAT?

SOMETHING AT THE DOOR...

17

107

OH, NO, N-NO!

I...I SHOT *TARZAN!*

MERCI, LE BON DIEU!

THE BULLET STRUCK BUT A GLANCING BLOW!

I...COULD NOT...DESERT YOU, MON AMI...

Tears of relief well in the Frenchman's eyes as he ministers to the wounded ape-man...

I-I AM FINE, D'ARNOT... IT IS NOTHING, DO NOT WORRY...

NOTHING, YOU SAY? I MIGHT HAVE *KILLED* YOU...

BUT, HERE, MY FRIEND! THIS LETTER MAY HELP ATONE FOR MY *FAUX PAS!*

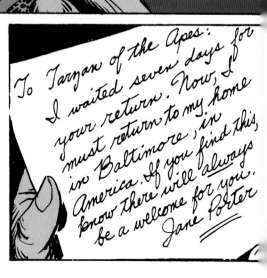

To Tarzan of the Apes: I waited seven days for your return. Now, I must return to my home in Baltimore, in America. If you find this, know there will always be a welcome for you.

Jane Porter

108

SHE *DID* WAIT!

D'ARNOT... *WHERE IS AMERICA?*

*S*EVERAL DAYS LATER THE TWO MEN START OUT FOR... *CIVILIZATION!*

WEEKS PASS, AS THEY JOURNEY THROUGH ENDLESS JUNGLES... WITH NO SIGN OF MAN OR ENCOUNTERING DANGER FROM WILD BEASTS!

I HAVE NEVER TRAVELED SO FAR FROM MY TRIBE, D'ARNOT...

IS IT MUCH FARTHER TO *BALTIMORE?*

INDEED, YES, MY FRIEND...

WEEKS SLIP INTO MONTHS... UNTIL, FINALLY...

TARZAN! WE HAVE ARRIVED! IT IS A *TRADING OUTPOST...*

I HAVE NEVER SEEN... SUCH *LARGE HOUSES!*

ARE THEY ENEMIES, D'ARNOT?

WHY DO THEY *RUN?*

NO, NO... IT IS JUST THAT NONE HAVE EVER SEEN A MAN SUCH AS YOU, *TARZAN!*

AT LEAST, NO *CIVILIZED* MAN!

19

SEVERAL WEEKS LATER...

THIS BOOK IS ONE I FOUND IN MY CABIN--A LONG TIME AGO--THE *ONLY* ONE I COULD *NEVER READ!* CAN YOU--?

LT. D'ARNOT SPEAKS...AS A DARK-HAIRED YOUNG GIANT LISTENS INTENTLY...

MAIS *OUI,* MON AMI...IT IS IN *FRENCH!*

IT IS ODD THAT THOUGH YOU *SPEAK* FRENCH AS WELL AS I...YOU CAN *READ* ONLY *ENGLISH!*

IT IS *TARZAN!*

READ IT TO ME, PLEASE,...FOR MANY YEARS I HAVE THOUGHT OF THE *STORY* THIS BOOK MA[Y] CONTAIN!

IT...IS A *DIARY*...WRITTEN BY *LORD GREY-STOKE!* TELLING OF HIS WIFE...AND *CHILD!*

YOU MUST BE THAT CHILD, *TARZAN!*

NO, D'ARNOT... THE *SKELETON* OF A *BABY* WAS FOUND IN THAT CABIN!

MY MOTHER WAS *KALA,* THE SHE-APE...

THAT *CANNOT BE!* YOU ARE A NORMAL *MAN,* TARZAN...

SEE HERE,...THE CHILD'S *FINGER-PRINTS* HAVE BEEN PRESSED ONTO THIS PAGE!

DIARY

FINGER-PRINTS?

YES, MY FRIEND... A MEANS OF *IDENTIFICA-TION!* ONE THAT NEVER CHANGES, THROUGHOU[T] ONE'S LIFE!

As the two friends step out into the compound...

A MAD-MAN... RUNNING AMOK!

HE DOES SEEM A BIT PERTURBED, MON AMI!

MINUTES LATER A GRATEFUL CONSTABULARY ARRIVES...

THANK YOU, M'SIEUR TARZAN! YOU WILL BE REWARDED FOR YOUR BRAVE ACTION!

NO, NO... IT WAS NOTHING--

A REWARD WILL HELP PAY FOR PORTAGE TO AMERICA!

AS YOU SAY, D'ARNOT!

21

PARIS... SEVERAL WEEKS LATER...

TARZAN...I WILL SEND YOU A REPORT OF THE RESULTS CONCERNING THE FINGERPRINTS WE FOUND IN GREYSTOKE'S DIARY!

D'ARNOT...YOU HAVE BEEN A GOOD FRIEND!

TOMORROW, I LEAVE FOR AMERICA...TO FIND JANE!

ABOARD THE SHIP BOUND FOR AMERICA, TARZAN LEARNS TO SPEAK ENGLISH FROM HIS FELLOW PASSENGERS...

BALTIMORE, U.S.A....

MISS PORTER, A MR.--ER-TARZAN TO SEE YOU!

JANE...

WHO--? IT-IT'S YOU! THE W-WILD MAN...?

TARZAN! I SAY, OLD MAN...GOOD TO SEE YOU AGAIN!

YOU KNOW... MY FIANCE, WILLIAM CLAYTON! HE IS NOW LORD GREYSTOKE!

I DO HOPE YOU CAN STAY FOR THE OCCASION, OLD MAN...

AND...WE ARE TO BE MARRIED IN A FORT-NIGHT!

AFTER ALL... WE OWE YOU OUR LIVES!

PARDON...CABLEGRAM FOR MR. TARZAN!

CABLEGRAM

FINGERPRINTS PROVE
LORD GREYSTOKE
CONGRATULATION
D'ARNO

YES, TARZAN... T REALLY TOOK A BIT OF PERSUASION BEFORE JANE FINALLY PROMISED TO BE MY WIFE!

BUT, TELL ME, OLD MAN... HOW *DID* YOU GET INTO THAT JUNGLE, ANYWAY?

TARZAN STARES AT THE MAN WHO IS GOING TO MARRY THE WOMAN HE LOVES... THE MAN WHO HAS *TARZAN'S* TITLE AND ESTATES!

*H*E HAS THE PROOF OF HERITAGE IN HIS POCKET! ONE WORD FROM THE TALL, DARK-HAIRED GIANT COULD ALTER THE LIVES OF *ALL THREE PEOPLE!*

*S*LOWLY...DELIBERATELY... HE ANSWERS CLAYTON'S QUESTION...

I...WAS *BORN* IN THE JUNGLE! MY MOTHER... WAS AN *APE!* I NEVER KNEW *WHO MY FATHER WAS!*

KLAXTON... DO YOU MEAN TO SAY THAT THE MAN WE SAW HERE IN THE JUNGLE... IS THE *SAME* TARZAN?

THE NATIVES SAY HE'S A *GOD!* AGELESS... ALL-POWERFUL...

THEN... WE *MUST* FIND THIS *APE-MAN!*

*H*E WILL KNOW OF MY FATHER... LOST IN THIS JUNGLE...

LOOKIT HERE, MISS... EVEN IF I *COULD--* I *WOULDN'T!*

*S*UDDENLY...

23

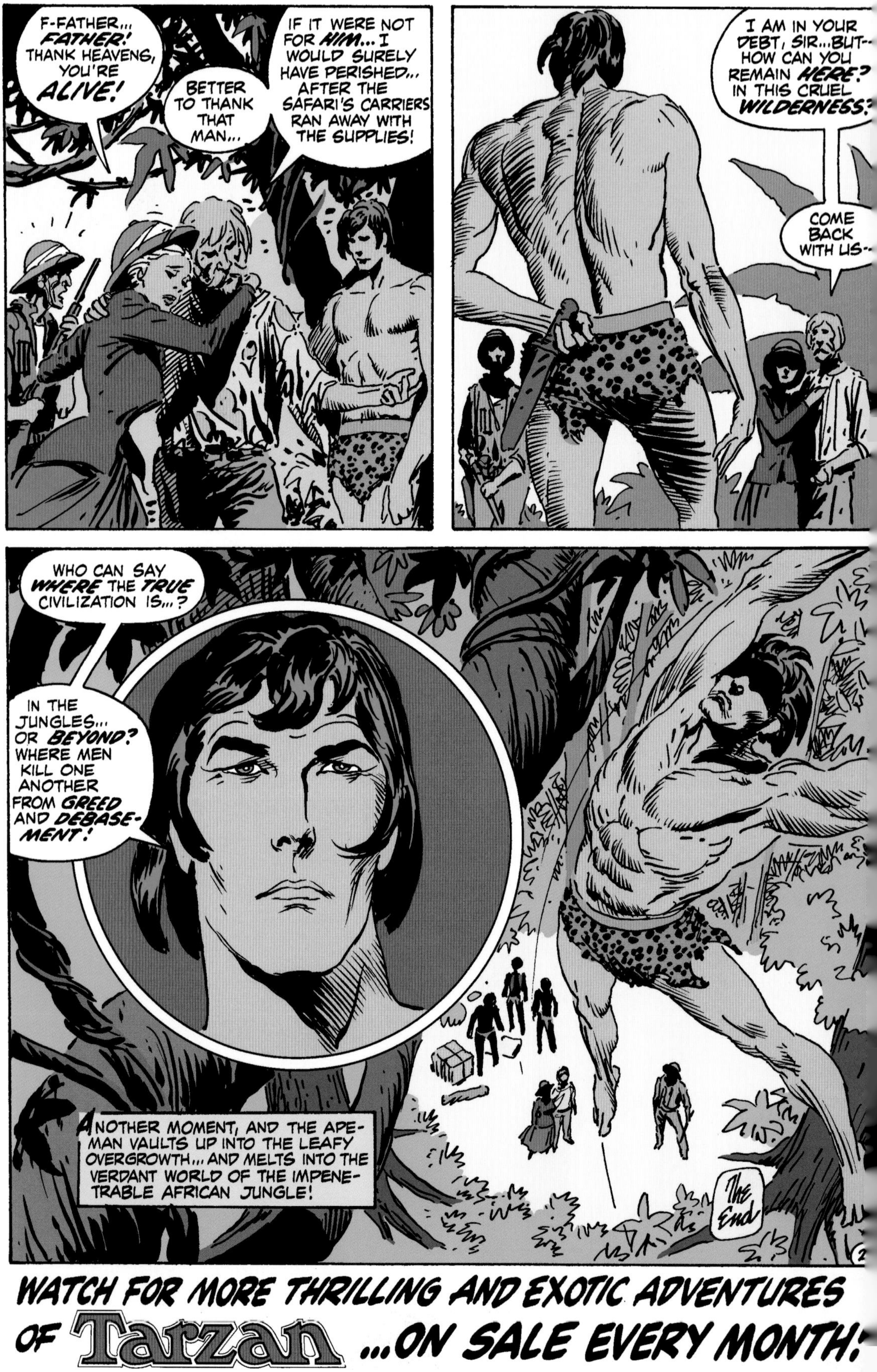
F-FATHER... FATHER! THANK HEAVENS, YOU'RE ALIVE!
BETTER TO THANK THAT MAN...
IF IT WERE NOT FOR HIM... I WOULD SURELY HAVE PERISHED... AFTER THE SAFARI'S CARRIERS RAN AWAY WITH THE SUPPLIES!
I AM IN YOUR DEBT, SIR... BUT-- HOW CAN YOU REMAIN HERE? IN THIS CRUEL WILDERNESS?
COME BACK WITH US--
WHO CAN SAY WHERE THE TRUE CIVILIZATION IS...?
IN THE JUNGLES... OR BEYOND? WHERE MEN KILL ONE ANOTHER FROM GREED AND DEBASEMENT!
ANOTHER MOMENT, AND THE APE-MAN VAULTS UP INTO THE LEAFY OVERGROWTH... AND MELTS INTO THE VERDANT WORLD OF THE IMPENETRABLE AFRICAN JUNGLE!
The End
WATCH FOR MORE THRILLING AND EXOTIC ADVENTURES OF Tarzan ...ON SALE EVERY MONTH!

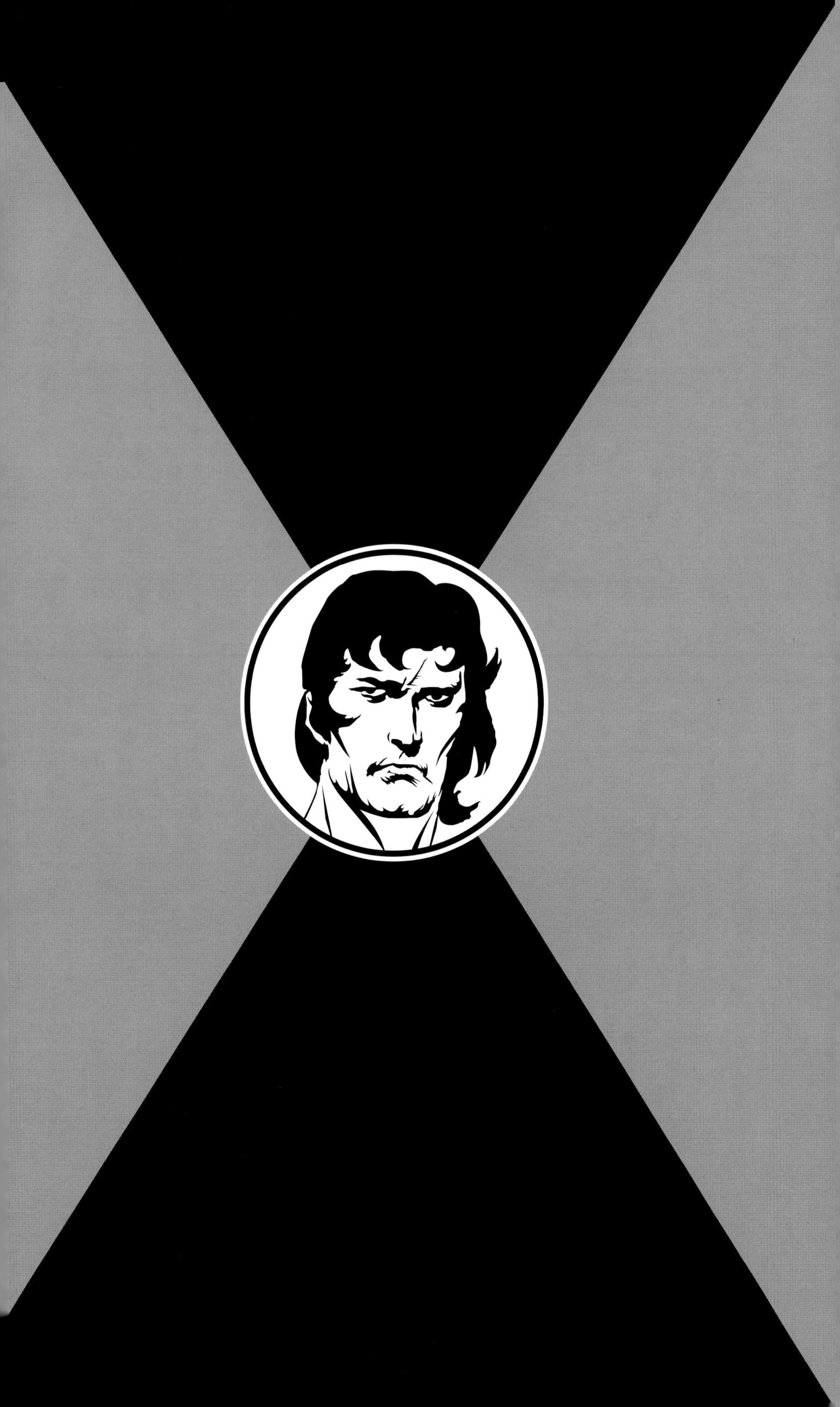

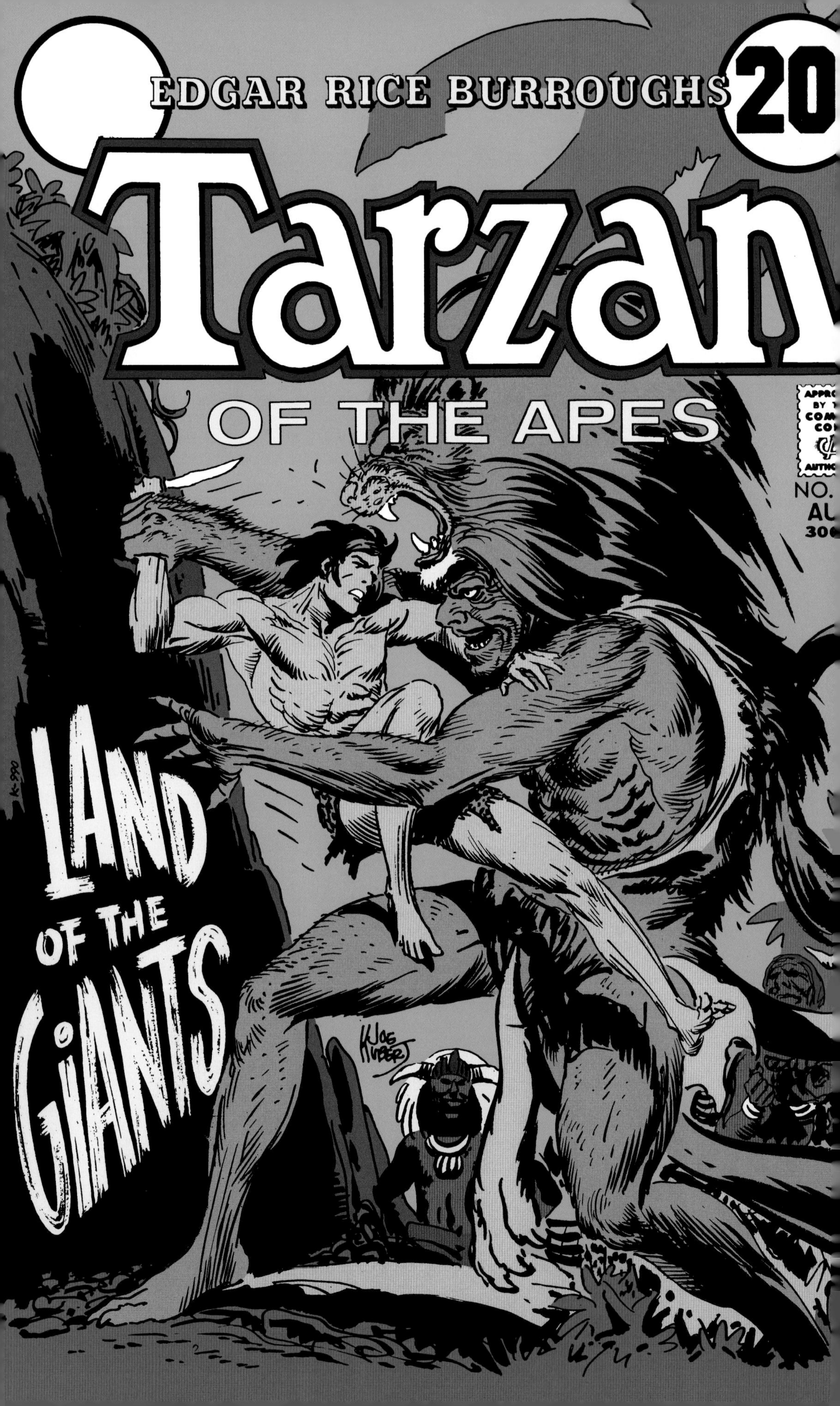

EDGAR RICE BURROUGHS
20
Tarzan
OF THE APES
NO.
AU
LAND OF THE GIANTS
JOE KUBERT

DEEP IN THE UNCHARTED *AFRICAN JUNGLE*...WARM TROPICAL AIR HANGS LIKE A SOFT WEIGHT...WITH NO BREEZE TO MOVE LEAF OR BRANCH...

THE MID-DAY SUN HAS STILLED EVEN *YOUR* CHATTERING LITTLE *MANU!*

A COOL SWIM WILL BE WELCOME!

AS THE SUN-BRONZED FIGURE PLUMMETS TOWARD THE JUNGLE STREAM BELOW...SCALE-LIDDED EYES *WATCH*...UNBLINKING! TAPERED BODIES SLIDE INTO THE WATER...INTENT ON FILLING THEIR *EMPTY BELLIES!*

1

SLICING INTO THE WATER LIKE A KNIFE, HE PLUMBS THE COOL DEPTHS...

OVERHEAD, IN THE TREETOPS..."*TARZAN, TARZAN!*" THE MONKEYS SCREAM A WARNING TO THE *APE-MAN*...

FACING THE SAURIANS' ATTACK WITHOUT HESITATION, THE *JUNGLE LORD* CLAMPS AN ARM OF STEEL AROUND THE FIRST CROCODILE'S SCALY NECK...AND DRIVES HIS SHARP BLADE AGAIN AND AGAIN INTO THE TWISTING, THRASHING BEAST!

Tarzan
"LAND OF THE GIANTS"

②

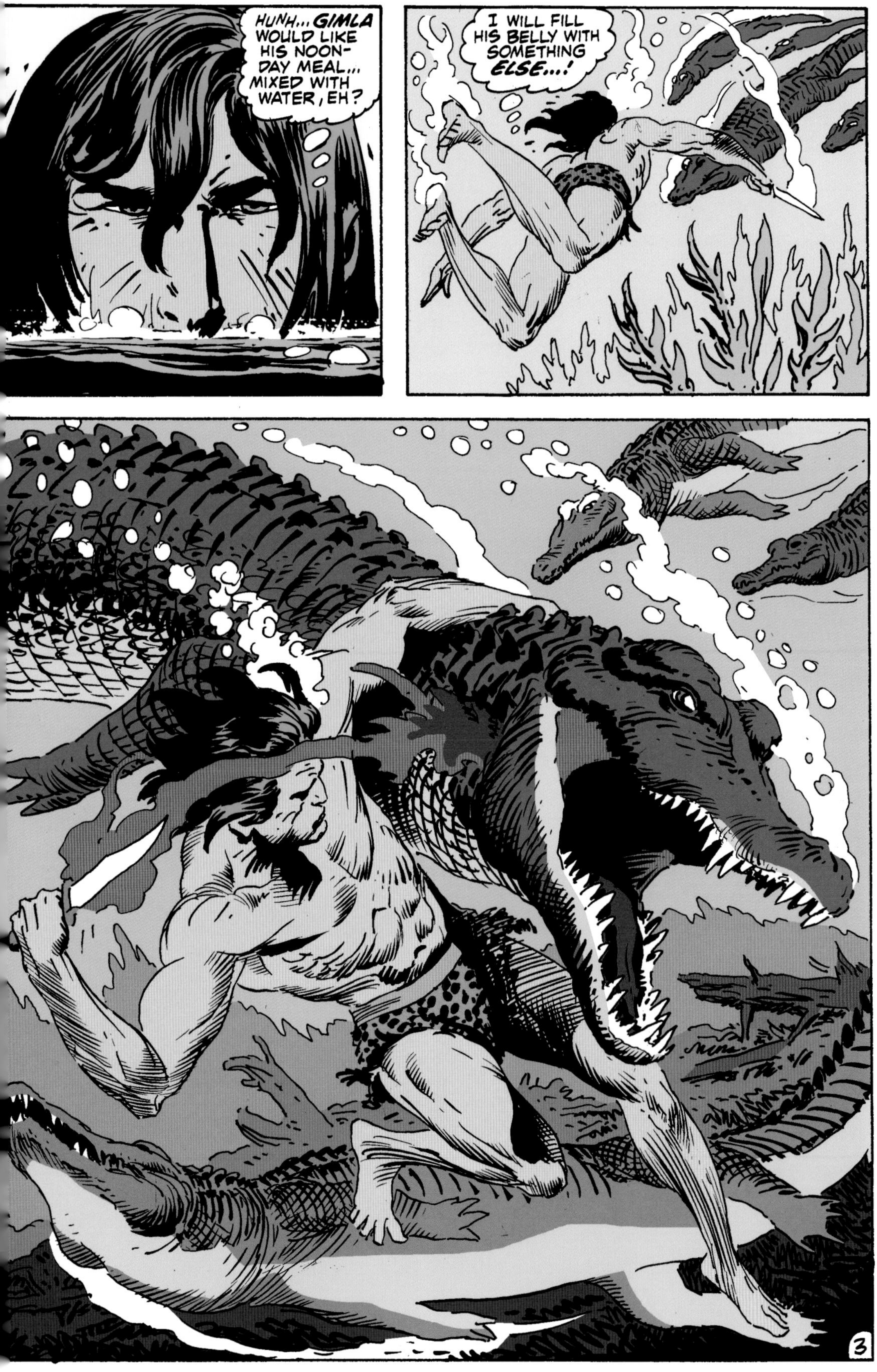
HUNH... GIMLA WOULD LIKE HIS NOON-DAY MEAL... MIXED WITH WATER, EH?
I WILL FILL HIS BELLY WITH SOMETHING ELSE...!
3

STRICKEN, THE DYING REPTILE'S BLOOD SPREADS QUICKLY IN THE WATER...ATTRACTING HIS HUNGRY BROTHERS...

SURFACING FURTHER DOWN-STREAM, *TARZAN* GULPS THE SWEET AIR...AND REALIZES A NEW *DANGER!*

RAPIDS!

CAUGHT IN THE SEETHING WATERS...

UNHH!

THE *APE-KING'S* UNCONSCIOUS FORM IS BORNE SWIFTLY ALONG THE SURGING RAPIDS... OVER A SERIES OF ROCKY WATERFALLS... TOSSED LIKE A LEAF IN A STORM!

THEN...HE IS SWEPT INTO A QUIET LAKE...ON THE FLOOR OF A *MYSTERIOUS VALLEY!*

HO, *TITANUS!* LOOK...ON THE WATER...

A MAN...FROM THE *OUTSIDE WORLD...*

IF HE IS LIKE THE *OTHERS*... WE SHOULD LET HIM *DROWN!*

NO, *TITANUS*... WE ARE NOT *SAVAGE MURDERERS!*

*M*OMENTS LATER POWERFUL ARMS LIFT *TARZAN* INTO A STRANGE CANOE...

PERHAPS HE WILL DIE, *TITANUS*... THAT WOULD BE LESS TROUBLESOME...FOR *ALL OF US!*

HE IS NOT BADLY HURT....

SEE? HE IS AWAKENING!

SUDDENLY...

STAND ASIDE, YOU OXEN! WHO IS THAT? WHY ARE YOU HELPING AN *OUTSIDER?*

*T*HE SMALL, DEFORMED MAN SCREAMS A SHRILL THREAT...

I HAVE WARNED YOU MORONS....*NO ONE* IS PERMITTED INTO THIS VALLEY! STAND *ASIDE!*

5

STAND ASIDE, I
SAID! HE MUST DIE! OR--
WOULD YOU SACRIFICE
YOUR OWN LIVES--
FOR THIS STRANGER?

IF YOU DON'T
MOVE...I'LL
KILL YOU
ALL!

WHA-
--UNH--
WH-WHERE
AM I...?

WITH THE IN-
STINCTIVE REFLEX
OF A JUNGLE
CREATURE
TARZAN LEAPS
INTO THE
TREES, AS...

SOMERSAULTING IN
MID-AIR, HE CATAPULTS
GROUNDWARD...

YOU'VE NO NEED
FOR THIS, MON
PETIT! YOU MAY
HURT YOUR-
SELF!

122

LEAVE... *NOW!* THE NEXT TIME WE MEET, I MAY NOT BE SO *GENTLE* WITH YOU!

YOU WOULD HAVE DONE BETTER TO *KILL ME...* BEFORE WE MEET AGAIN!

*A*S THE SMALL, MALEVOLENT FIGURE DISAPPEARS INTO THE BRUSH...

WHAT IS YOUR TRIBE? AND-- WHO IS THAT MAN?

WE ARE *KOLOSANS...* AND HIS NAME IS *MARTIUS KALBAN!*

WE ARE A PEACEFUL PEOPLE... LIVING IN THIS HIDDEN VALLEY, AWAY FROM THE OUTSIDE WORLD!

MARTIUS KALBAN SEEKS THE SECRET OF OUR SIZE AND STRENGTH! ALREADY HE HAS SLAIN SEVERAL WHO HAVE REFUSED TO AID HIM IN HIS SEARCH!

WHY DO YOU NOT *LEAVE* THIS VALLEY?

LOOK ABOUT YOU...

HUNH! THESE CANYON WALLS ARE SMOOTH AS *SAND!* THE *KOLOSANS* COULD NOT SCALE THEM... AND... *NEITHER CAN I!*

7

TARZAN'S ATTENTION IS CAUGHT BY A POWERFUL, MENACING ROAR...

NUMA!

MOMENTS BEFORE, THE EVIL DWARF MARTIUS HAD JOINED A BEAUTIFUL PARTNER...

WHERE IS YOUR RIFLE, MARTIUS?

BROKEN... BY A WILD-MAN...

THEN...

IT'S... IT'S A LION!

GIVE ME YOUR RIFLE... BEFORE IT ATTACKS!

NUMA...ATTACKING THAT GIRL! I HAVE NEVER SEEN A LION OF SUCH SIZE!

M-MARTIUS... COME BACK! DON'T...LEAVE ME...

LION AND APE-MAN SPRING AT THE SAME PRECISE MOMENT... AS MUSCLES AND TENDONS REACT LIKE STEEL CORDS IN MAN AND BEAST!

THE HUGE FELINE LEAPS AND SPINS IN A VAIN ATTEMPT TO DISLODGE *TARZAN...*

THE *APE-MAN* CLINGS TO THE GREAT MANE... PLUNGING HIS KNIFE DEEP INTO THE CREATURE'S VITALS!

TERRIBLE, HEART-STOPPING MOMENTS LATER...

WHO ARE YOU? WHAT IS YOUR CONNECTION TO THE MAN *MARTIUS KALBAN?*

MY NAME IS *OLGA STERN!* I AM *DR. KALBAN'S* ASSISTANT!

HE...RAN AWAY! LEFT ME TO BE *KILLED* BY THAT LION! YOU MUST HELP ME--

L-LOOK... *BEHIND YOU!*

TARZAN WHIRLS... AND FINDS HIMSELF FACE-TO-FACE WITH A *MONSTER GORILLA!*

9

REMAIN SILENT... *DO NOT MOVE!* PERHAPS... I CAN SPEAK TO HIM!

"*I* AM *TARZAN,* KING OF THE APES! I WANT NO FIGHT... I APPROACH AS A FRIEND!"

"*YOU* SPEAK MY TONGUE, *WHITE SKIN!* GO, THEN... *AS A FRIEND!*"

WALK SLOWLY... BESIDE ME! THEY WILL NOT HARM YOU!

MY KNEES ARE TREMBLING...

PROF. KALBAN DISCOVERED THAT LIFE IN THIS HIDDEN VALLEY GROWS TO *TREMENDOUS SIZE!*

HE WANTS TO USE THAT SECRET ON *HIMSELF!*

HOW DID YOU TWO COME *INTO* THIS VALLEY? HOW WILL YOU GET *OUT?*

BEFORE THE GIRL CAN REPLY...A *KOLOSAN* CATAPULTS ONTO *TARZAN'S* BACK...

CARRYING THE *APE-MAN* AS IF HE WERE A BABE-IN-ARMS, THE *KOLOSAN* RACES INTO THE DENSE JUNGLE...

TO STAY WITH THAT WOMAN... WOULD MEAN YOUR *DEATH!*

THIS IS MY VILLAGE! THE CHIEFTAINS ARE GOING TO THE *FORBIDDEN FOUNTAIN!*

COME!

IT WILL BE OF INTEREST TO SEE *WHY* THE FOUNTAIN IS SAID TO BE *FORBIDDEN!*

ENTER... YOU WHO CARRY THE *SACRED LION SKIN...* AT YOUR *OWN* PERIL!

As *TARZAN* STEPS INTO THE GLOOMY EDIFICE...

LOOK CLOSELY, OUTSIDER... AND YOU WILL SEE THAT WHICH THE CRUEL DWARF WOULD GIVE HIS *SOUL* TO LEARN!

11

127

HIDDEN FROM THEIR SIGHT, *MARTIUS KALBAN* HAS SPIED ON THE KOLOSANS' PROCESSION...

THIS MUST BE THEIR *HOLIEST PLACE*... WHERE THEY KEEP THE SECRET OF *GROWTH!*

WE PRAY THAT THESE *FORBIDDEN WATERS* WILL REMAIN EVER IN THIS FOUNT... AND NEVER FLOW IN OUR BELOVED VALLEY!

FOR WE KNOW THAT *ANY* EXCESS... MAY LEAD TO *DOOM AND DESTRUCTION!*

WHOEVER DRINKS FROM THESE WATERS GROWS INSTANTLY *HUGE AND STRONG!* BUT... MAY WELL LOSE HIS *SOUL!*

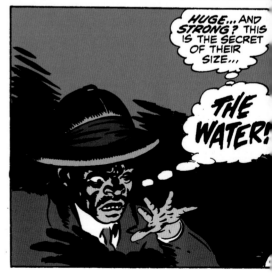

HUGE... AND *STRONG?* THIS IS THE SECRET OF THEIR SIZE...

THE WATER!

128

DRIVEN BY HIS INSANE QUEST, *KALGAN* RUSHES TO THE FOUNTAIN BEFORE ANY HAND CAN STOP HIM...

MIRACULOUSLY, THE SMALL, TWISTED BODY ASSUMES A MONSTROUS TRANSFORMATION...

LOOK! HE HAS EVEN DONNED THE SACRED LION SKIN!

WE MUST *STOP* HIM...

IT IS WELL YOUR COMRADES HOLD YOU BACK ...OR *I WOULD* CRUSH YOU LIKE A FLEA!

I AM RULER OF *ALL BEASTS AND MEN!*

THOSE WHO WOULD DENY ME... *WILL BE TORN ASUNDER!*

13

129

NOW I WILL BRING THE WATER'S POWER TO THE VILLAGERS!

HEE HEEEE HEE HEEE

AWE-STRUCK, THE *KOLOSANS* LISTEN TO THE WILD FIGURE ADORNED IN LION SKIN...

ONE SIP OF THIS LIQUID, AND YOU WILL ENTER MY WORLD OF *MASTER ME—*

DRINK

HALTINGLY, SOME GRASPING HANDS REACH FOR THE *FORBIDDEN WATER*...

YOU- YOU HAVE TURNED THEM INTO *SOMETHING INHUMAN!*

YES... SOMETHING *ABOVE* HUMAN!

GOD-LIKE!

WE WILL MAKE AN EXAMPLE OF OUR POWER...

KILL THE OLD CHIEFS!

UNABLE TO CONTROL THEIR OWN MINDS, THE MONSTER-KOLOSANS ACT...

...TEARING AND CRUSHING MEN AND BUILDINGS!

OLGA! SO... YOU HAVE FOUND ME! LOOK AT ME!

NO MORE THE TWISTED DWARF... BUT-- MORE POWERFUL THAN THE STRONGEST MAN!

WHY DO YOU RUN? DO I FRIGHTEN YOU?

JUST THEN... A SMALL, LITHE FIGURE EMERGES FROM THE FOREST...

LEAVE THE GIRL ALONE!

THIS IS THE GREATEST IRONY OF ALL! NOW, LITTLE MAN... YOU ARE THE DWARF!

H-HELP ME,,, HE HAS GONE *MAD!*

WHAT CAN A *PIGMY* DO,,, AGAINST *GODS?*

SEIZE HIM!

CRUSH HIM!

*T*WISTING OUT OF THE GIANT'S GRASP,,,*TARZAN* STABS THE HEEL OF HIS FOOT INTO THE BASE OF THE BEHEMOTH'S WINDPIPE,,,

*A*NOTHER SECOND, AND A STUNNING BLOW IS DRIVEN AGAINST *KALBAN'S* UNPROTECTED CHIN!

HOLD TIGHTLY TO ME,,,

THESE GREAT CLODS ARE STRONG,,, BUT THEY MOVE LIKE *KOTA,* THE TORTOISE!

TARZAN EASILY OUTDISTANCES HIS PURSUERS... THEN...

TELL ME, QUICKLY... DO YOU KNOW HOW TO GET *OUT* OF THIS VALLEY?

Y-YES...

BY *AIR-PLANE!* I PILOTED IT... LANDED... ON A CLEARING BEYOND THOSE TREES!

RACING THROUGH THE FOREST...

THERE IT IS... JUST AS I TOLD YOU!

HEE HEE HEEE... I *KNEW* YOU WOULD LEAD HIM HERE, OLGA!

MARTIUS KALBAN!

NOW, JUNGLE MAN... I WILL DESTROY YOU *MYSELF!*

THE WATER YOU DRANK HAS ALREADY DESTROYED YOUR *MIND!*

AFTER YOU ARE *DISPATCHED*, I WILL ALLOW *OLGA* TO DRINK THE SAME WATER... AND REIGN HERE WITH ME AS MY *QUEEN!*

YOU WILL FIND YOURSELF ONE OF THE *MINIONS OF HADES*... MARTIUS KALBAN!

I AWAIT YOU!

17

MONSTROUS GIANT AND MAN OF THE JUNGLE CLASH...EACH KNOWING THAT *DEATH* WILL DECIDE THE VICTOR!

HEEE HEE... YOUR FEEBLE EFFORTS WILL DO YOU *NO GOOD*--

*S*HIFTING HIS WEIGHT SUDDENLY, *TARZAN* REVERSES LEVERAGE,... AND USES THE MONSTER'S OWN WEIGHT AND MOMENTUM,...

*L*IGHTNING-FAST, THE *APE-MAN* CLAMPS A VISE-LIKE GRIP AROUND HIS ADVERSARY'S THROAT,...

*F*INALLY, HE RELEASES *MARTIUS KALBAN* WHOSE LIFELESS BODY SINKS TO THE GROUND,...

TARZAN! KALBAN... IS... CHANGING!

BEFORE THEIR VERY EYES, THE LIFELESS BODY RESUMES ITS ORIGINAL SHAPE... BEFORE TASTING THE *FORBIDDEN WATERS!*

THE WATER'S EFFECT WAS *NOT* PERMANENT! ALL THOSE WHO HAVE DRUNK IT... WILL RETURN TO *NORMAL!*

IT'S TIME FOR *US* TO LEAVE THIS PLACE, OLGA...

*S*OON, THE TWIN ENGINES WHINE AND COUGH INTO ROARING LIFE...

JUST A FEW MINUTES... UNTIL THE ENGINES WARM UP, *TARZAN!*

NEARBY, THE GIANT GORILLA *TARZAN* MET ON HIS ARRIVAL... CHANCES UPON *KALBAN'S* WATER CANTEEN... *AND DRINKS!*

*T*HE TRANS- FORMATION IS IMMEDIATE... AND *HORRIBLE!*

19

135

DRIVEN MAD BY THE WATER...READY TO ATTACK *ANYTHING*... THE GIANT ANTHROPOID LUMBERS AFTER THE PLANE...

SOMETHING'S WRONG WITH THE PLANE! IT ISN'T RESPONDING TO THE CONTROLS...

LIKE A DRUNKEN BIRD, THE AIRSHIP LURCHES INTO THE SKY...

TARZAN... ON THE WING! A GIANT GORILLA!

HE'LL PULL US *ALL DOWN!*

FURIOUSLY, THE GORILLA SCREAMS A CHALLENGE...

THE *APE-MAN* ANSWERS... BY CRAWLING ONTO THE PLANE'S FUSELAGE!

"HUNH!... YOU ARE MY *ENEMY!* I FIGHT... I *KILL!*"

THE WATER HAS DESTROYED HIS MIND... HE WILL NOT LISTEN TO REASON!

I MUST DISLODGE HIM... BEFORE HE DESTROYS THE PLANE!

WITH NO THOUGHT FOR HIS OWN SAFETY, THE *JUNGLE LORD* THROWS HIMSELF AT THE CRAZED BEAST....

UNH! GOT TO... HOLD ON...

21

HE...HE PUSHED THE APE OFF, BUT--

TARZAN FELL--

I'M ALL RIGHT, OLGA...JUST TOOK THE *LONG* WAY 'ROUND!

TH-THANK HEAVENS YOU'RE *SAFE!*

HEAD THE PLANE IN AN *EASTERLY* DIRECTION...WHILE I PUT ON A *PARACHUTE!*

WHA-WHAT ARE YOU GOING TO DO?

THE JUNGLES BEYOND THAT ESCARPMENT IS MY HOME! I'M GOING BACK... *NOW!*

GOODBYE, OLGA...

BUT-- YOU *CAN'T--*

*B*EFORE ANOTHER WORD COULD BE UTTERED, *TARZAN* DID!

NOT LONG AFTER...

HUNH...ANOTHER WARM DAY...

NO, LITTLE *MANU*...I AM *NOT* GOING SWIMMING *TODAY!*

THE END

NEXT ISSUE ON SALE ON OR ABOUT *JULY 25TH*

2

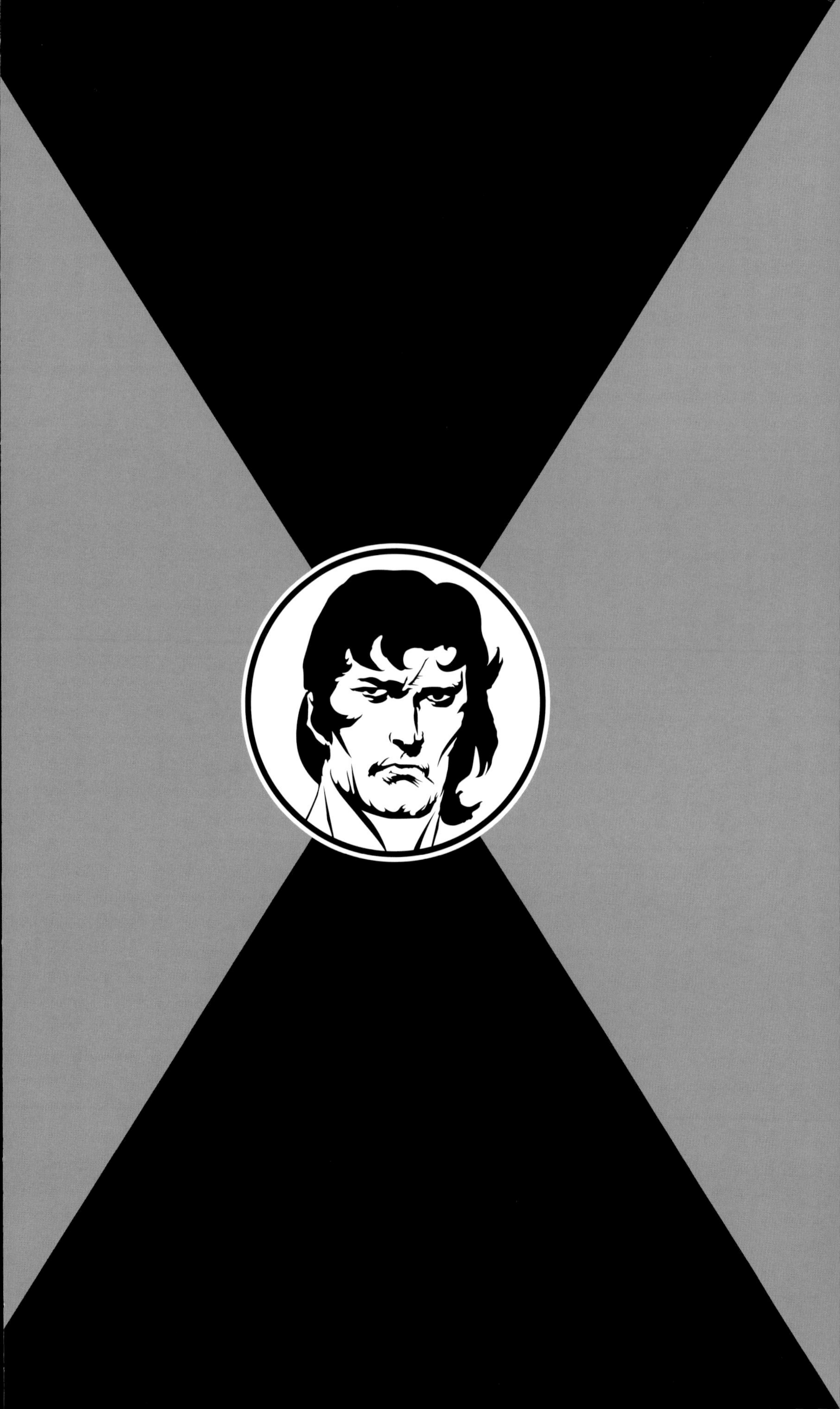

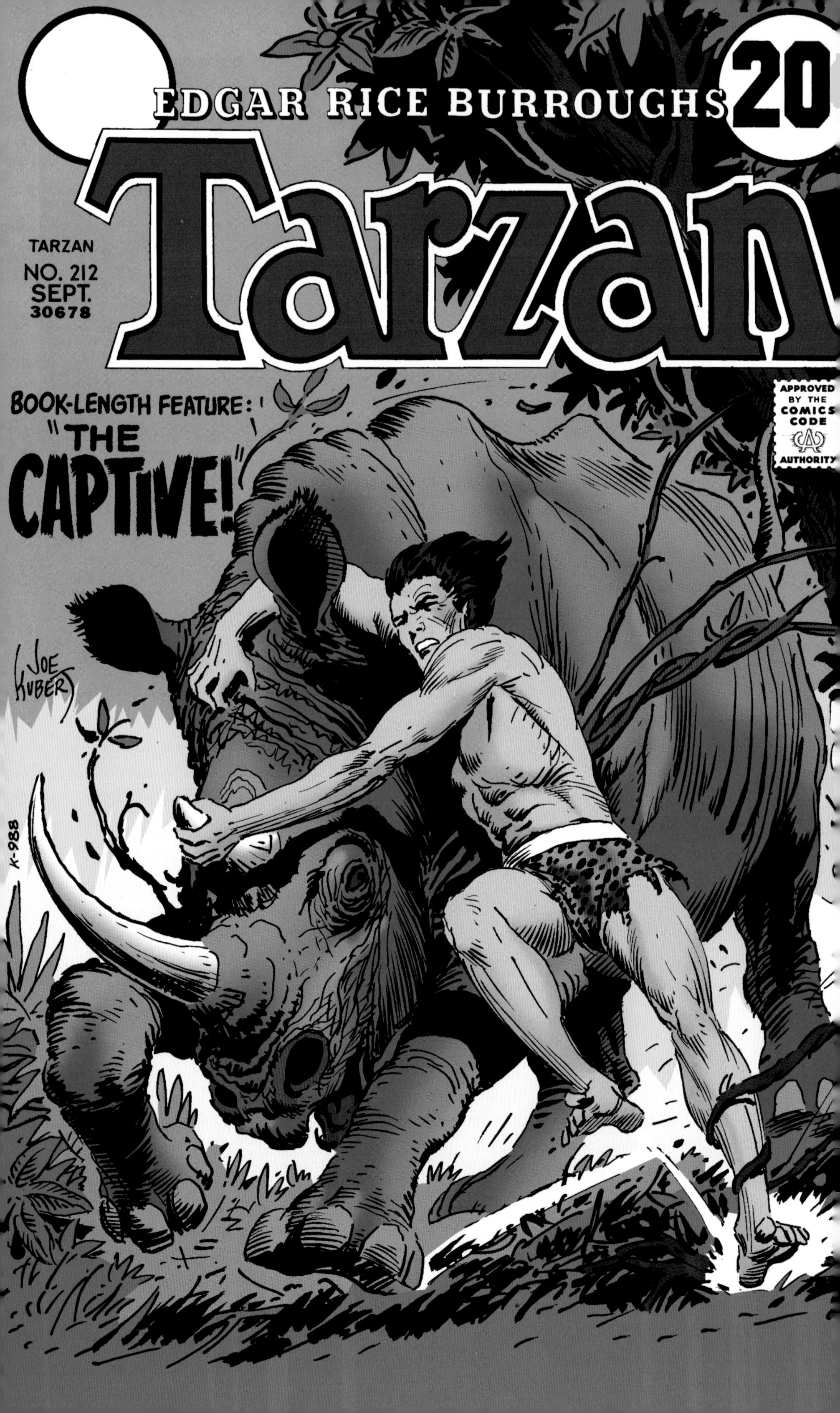

EDGAR RICE BURROUGHS
20¢
Tarzan
TARZAN
NO. 212
SEPT.
30678
APPROVED BY THE COMICS CODE AUTHORITY
BOOK-LENGTH FEATURE:
"THE CAPTIVE!"
JOE KUBERT
K-988

OON AFTER YOUNG *TARZAN* SLEW *KERCHAK* AND THUS BECAME KING OF THE GREAT APES, AND *KALA* (HIS APE FOSTER-MOTHER) *WAS KILLED BY THE TRIBE OF M'BONGA,* THIS STORY HAPPENED! STAY... AND I WILL TELL IT TO YOU...

K JOE KUBERT

IN THE STIFLING HUMID HEAT OF THE SHADE-DAPPLED AFRICAN JUNGLE... BLACK MEN DIG... SWEAT GLISTENING ON THEIR NAKED BODIES...

NOT FAR, *WAPPI,* THE LONG-HORNED ANTE-LOPE STOPS WARILY... NOSTRILS FLARED... TO CATCH MAN'S HEAVY SCENT!

EVEN REGAL *NUMA,* THE LION, MAKES A WIDE CIRCLE TO SHUN CONTACT WITH THE *GOMANGANI!*...

IN THE RIVER NEARBY, *DURO,* THE HIPPOPOTAMUS, SNORTS,... THE ACTIVITY ON LAND DOES *NOT* CONCERN HIM!

K-993

1

HIGH OVERHEAD, A MOTIONLESS FIGURE WATCHES THE ACTIVITY BELOW...

A HOLE...BUT-- FOR WHAT *PURPOSE?*

AND--*WHY* DO THEY PLANT *POINTED STICKS* INSIDE?

HOURS LATER... THEIR LABORS DONE, THE NATIVES DEPART...

TARZAN SURVEYS THEIR WORK MORE CLOSELY...

HUNH! FIRST, THEY *DIG* A HOLE...THEN-- COVER IT WITH TWIGS AND LEAVES! IT... IS... *STRANGE!*

HE *APE-MAN* LEAPS INTO THE TREES...TO RACE ACROSS THE VAST, DIZZYING HEIGHTS OF HIS JUNGLE HOME...

I WILL FIND *TANTOR*...AND TELL HIM OF WHAT I HAVE SEEN!

2

Tarzan

"THE CAPTIVE!"

BASED ON *EDGAR RICE BURROUGHS'* *"JUNGLE TALES OF TARZAN!"*

"HO, TANTOR...
DO NOT BE STARTLED!
FOR ONE OF YOUR
SIZE AND STRENGTH...
YOU FRIGHTEN
TOO EASILY!"

OF ALL THE JUNGLE'S POPULATION, *TANTOR*, THE ELEPHANT, HOLDS *TARZAN'S* AFFECTION! BETWEEN THEM EXISTS A BOND OF UNDER-STANDING THAT HAS GROWN WITH THE PASSING OF TIME...

"...AND THEN--THEY COVERED THE HOLE WITH TWIGS AND LEAVES--AND *LEFT!*"

TARZAN IS NOT REALLY CERTAIN THAT *TANTOR* CAN TELL THE MEANING OF HIS WORDS...

YOU AND I, WE DO NOT SHARE THE TONGUE OF THE GREAT APES, *TANTOR*...

BUT-- OUR *THOUGHTS* SPEAK AS ONE!

SINCE THE DEATH OF MY MOTHER, *KALA*...I FEEL CLOSEST TO *TANTOR!*

"FAREWELL, *TANTOR*... I SHALL VISIT YOU AGAIN!"

TANTOR'S REPLY IS A LOW, RUMBLING SIGH...AS HE PICKS ANOTHER TENDER GREEN!

LATER...WITH THE TRIBE OF THE *GREAT APES*...

I *STILL* CANNOT REASON *WHY* A HOLE WAS DUG? AND WHY--

HUNH!

DRUMS OF THE GO-MANGANI!

AND--*TANTOR!* SCREAMING IN FRIGHT!

INSTANTLY, THE EXPLANATIONS ARE CLEARLY DEFINED IN THE *JUNGLE MAN'S* MIND!

TANTOR IS IN PERIL...OF... HIS *LIFE!*

5

145

I MUST FLY LIKE *USHA*, THE WIND... BEFORE *TANTOR* FALLS INTO THE PIT... *ONTO THE POINTED STICKS!*

"WHERE DOES TARZAN GO?"

"WHO KNOWS? HE IS NOT LIKE US! HIS MIND IS... PECULIAR!"

THE GROUND TREMBLES... *TANTOR* IS NEAR!

I MUST LEAVE THE TREES... AND TRAVEL THROUGH THIS CLEARING OF TALL GRASS!

S WIFTLY, THE *JUNGLE LORD* MAKES HIS WAY OVER AN UNCHARTED AERIAL PATHWAY...

HUNH! BIRDS... *BUTO'S BIRDS!*

AND... *BUTO* WILL *NOT* BE FAR BEHIND!

ALERTED BY THE STARTLED FLIGHT OF EVER-PRESENT LITTLE BIRDS WHO FEED ON THE BUGS IMBEDDED IN HIS THICK HIDE...

...BUTO THE RHINOCEROS, SPIES THE CAUSE OF THE DISTURBANCE!

"PERHAPS ANOTHER TIME I WILL STAY... TO FINISH THE GAME, STUPID BUTO!"

7

MEANWHILE, TANTOR FLEES FROM THE HOWLING NOISE-MAKERS CHASING HIM,...TOWARD CERTAIN, HORRIBLE **DEATH!**

BUT HIS PURSUERS CAN ALREADY SEE THE RICHES THE BEAST'S IVORY WOULD BRING,...AND HERD THE FRIGHTENED ANIMAL TO *THE PIT!*

GRIPPED BY FEAR AND PANIC, THE GIANT PACHYDERM SEEKS ONLY TO *ESCAPE*...

JUST THEN... A LITHE FIGURE HURTLES FROM THE TREES... AND LANDS AT THE *VERY EDGE* OF THE COVERED PIT!

"BACK, TANTOR... *BACK!*"

PROPELLED BY THE MOMENTUM OF HIS GREAT WEIGHT, *TANTOR* IS ALMOST UPON *TARZAN...*

TANTOR VEERS OFF AT THE LAST MOMENT... AND BURSTS THROUGH AN ALMOST SOLID WALL OF DENSE VEGETATION!

AS THE PIT'S EDGE CRUMBLES BENEATH HIS FOOT, *TARZAN FALLS...*

9

...INTO THE *PIT!*

IT-IT IS *MAGIC!*

WE CHASE AN *ELEPHANT*...

...AND FIND A *MAN!*

IT IS *MUNANGO KEEWATI*... THE EVIL ONE OF THE JUNGLE!

H-HE CHANGED HIMSELF... *FROM BEAST TO MAN,* CHIEF M'BONGA!

HE IS... STILL *ALIVE!*

TIE HIM *WELL!* WE WILL CARRY HIM TO THE VILLAGE!

M'BONGA... HAVE CARE. HE IS A *DEVIL!* KILL HIM *HERE*... *NOW!*

HIS POWER IS *GONE!* AND HIS DEATH WILL BE WITNESSED BY THE *ENTIRE TRIBE!*

TAKE HIM!

As darkness settles over the jungle, M'Bonga leads his procession triumphantly into the village compound...

DO NOT FEAR THE *EVIL ONE!* HE IS OUR *PRISONER!*

AND... HIS *DEATH* WILL BE RELISHED BY ALL! *TIE HIM TO THE POLES!*

SLOWLY, THE UNCONSCIOUS *APE-MAN* REVIVES... TO BE GREETED BY A SEA OF *HOSTILITY!*

HUNH! *TANTOR* IS SAVED... BUT-- *TARZAN* HAS TAKEN HIS PLACE!

I... AM *CAPTIVE!*

151

THICK, BLACK NIGHT SETTLES UPON THE JUNGLE-LAND... AS THE *THRUM-THRUM* OF DRUMS INCREASE IN TEMPO...

FROM THIS TIME FORTH, THE TRIBE OF *M'BONGA* WILL BE KNOWN AS THE *DEVIL'S SLAYER!*

SOUNDLESSLY, THE BOUND *LORD OF THE APES* SCANS THE ACTIVITY AS IT BUILDS TO A *FEVER-PITCH!* FIRES ARE STIRRED UNDER KETTLES OF BOILING WATER... AS THICKLY CALLOUSED FEET GYRATE WILDLY... AND THE OLD WOMEN STACK DRY TWIGS AT HIS FEET! COOLLY, THE CAPTIVE GAUGES THE *SHORT-LIVED,* BUT *PAIN-FILLED* FUTURE, THAT LAY IN STOR

FLAMING TORCHES GLEAM OFF EBONY BODIES... AS THE CHANTING, SWAYING CIRCLE CLOSES AROUND THE *CAPTIVE!*

THE INTENT IS CLEAR...AND THE END SEEMS UNAVOIDABLE!

ONE...*SMALL*... CHANCE! IF... ONLY HE *HEARS!* IF... ONLY HE *COMES!*

THROWING BACK HIS HEAD, *TARZAN* GIVES VENT TO THE TERRIFYING SCREAM OF THE *GREAT BULL-APE!*

AWESTRUCK...THE NATIVES STOP...AND *LISTEN...*

...BUT...ONLY THE SOFT RUSTLE OF HEAVY JUNGLE LEAVES IS HEARD...

NO USE! NONE TO HELP ME... BUT... *MYSELF!*

13

153

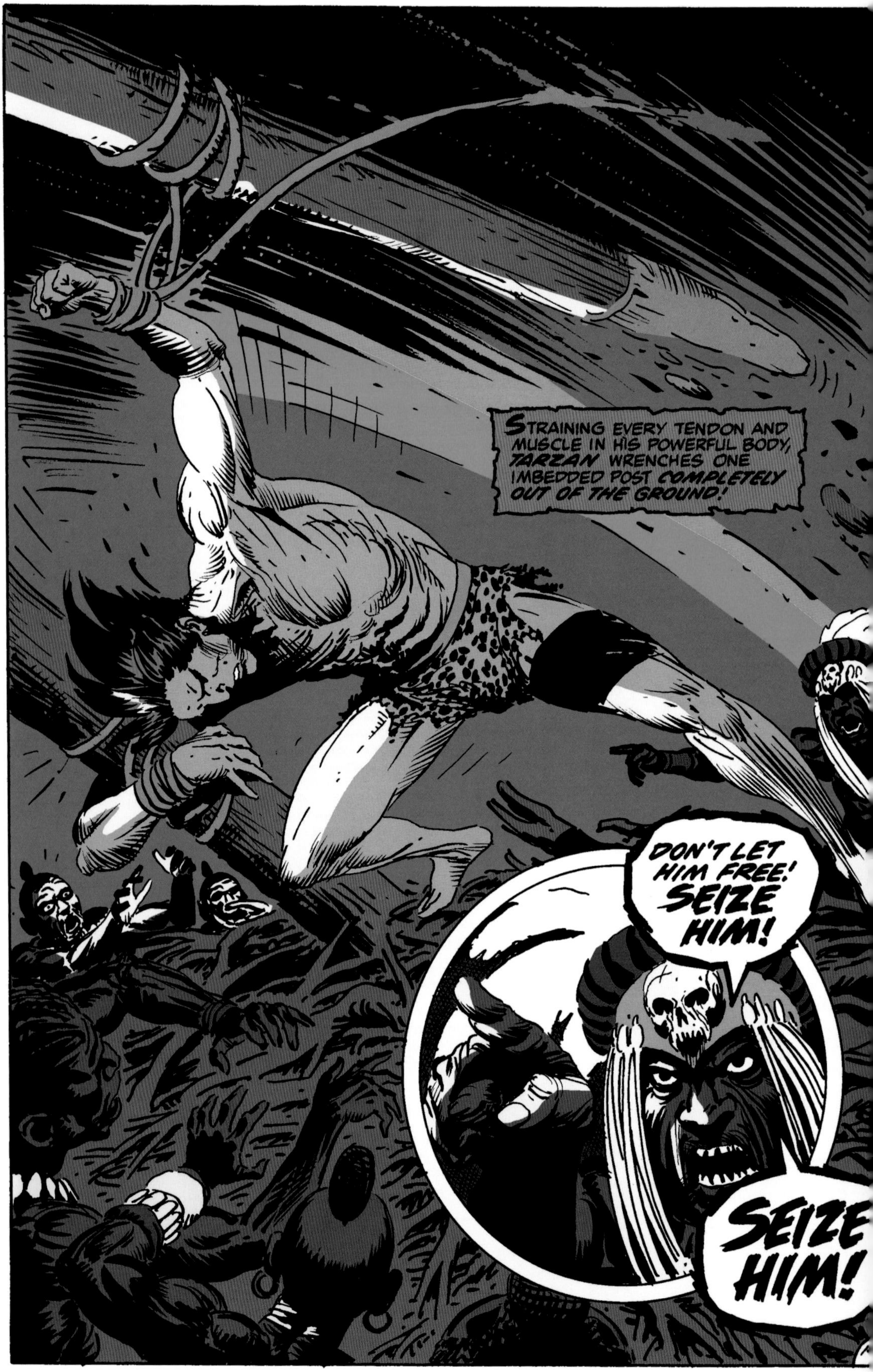
STRAINING EVERY TENDON AND MUSCLE IN HIS POWERFUL BODY, TARZAN WRENCHES ONE IMBEDDED POST COMPLETELY OUT OF THE GROUND!
DON'T LET HIM FREE! SEIZE HIM!
SEIZE HIM!

LIKE A TRAPPED, WILD BEAST, THE *APE-MAN* STRIKES BACK WITH TOOTH AND NAIL...

...TO NO AVAIL!

STAND BACK! I, M'BONGA, WILL MINISTER THE *DEATH BLOW!*

15

SUDDENLY, THE LOG WALL CIRCLING THE VILLAGE IS TORN AND RUPTURED WITH AN AWFUL FORCE... AS *TANTOR* TRUMPETS HIS ARRIVAL!

GENTLY, THE HUGE PACHYDERM LIFTS THE BLOODY AND BRUISED *JUNGLE LORD* ONTO HIS BROAD SKULL....

TANTOR'S TOWERING BULK HOVERS OVER THE STARTLED TRIBESMEN... AS THE SNAKE-LIKE TRUNK WEAVES, SELECTS, THEN FLINGS A HAPLESS "MISSILE"!

LOOK OUT FOR THE BOILING WATER! THE MONSTER UPSETS THE CAULDRONS...

RUN... RUN!

M'BONGA... THE WOODS-DEVIL HAS CAST A SPELL ON THE ELEPHANT!

WH-WHAT SHALL WE DO?

IN WORDLESS ANSWER, M'BONGA STEPS TOWARD THE GREAT, STAMPEDING CREATURE....

"NO, TANTOR! HE IS AN ENEMY... BUT, A BRAVE ONE! DO NOT HARM HIM...!"

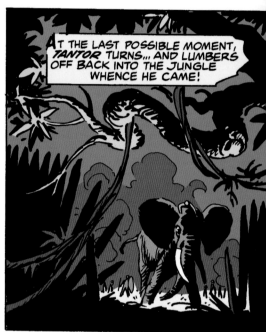

AT THE LAST POSSIBLE MOMENT, *TANTOR* TURNS... AND LUMBERS OFF BACK INTO THE JUNGLE WHENCE HE CAME!

YOU ARE THE *BRAVEST* CHIEF WHO EVER LIVED, *M'BONGA*... YOU CAUSED THE MONSTER TO *RUN AWAY!*

YOUR PRAISES WILL BE TOLD AND RETOLD THROUGH THE LAND!

WHY... *DID* THE BEAST... *NOT KILL ME?*

*LATER... IN THE MOONLIT SECLUSION OF *TARZAN'S* JUNGLE HOME...*

"THANK YOU, FRIEND TANTOR WE ARE TRUE BROTHERS, YOU AND I!"

—EPILOGUE—

THOSE WHO HAVE SPENT THE BETTER PART OF THEIR LIVES AMONG WILD ANIMALS... LEARNING THEIR HABITS... WILL DENY THAT *ANY* WILD ANIMAL WOULD HELP A MAN! BUT—*TARZAN* IS NOT A MERE MAN—BUT A FELLOW *JUNGLE BEAST!*

NEXT ISSUE ON SALE ON OR ABOUT AUG. 31ST.

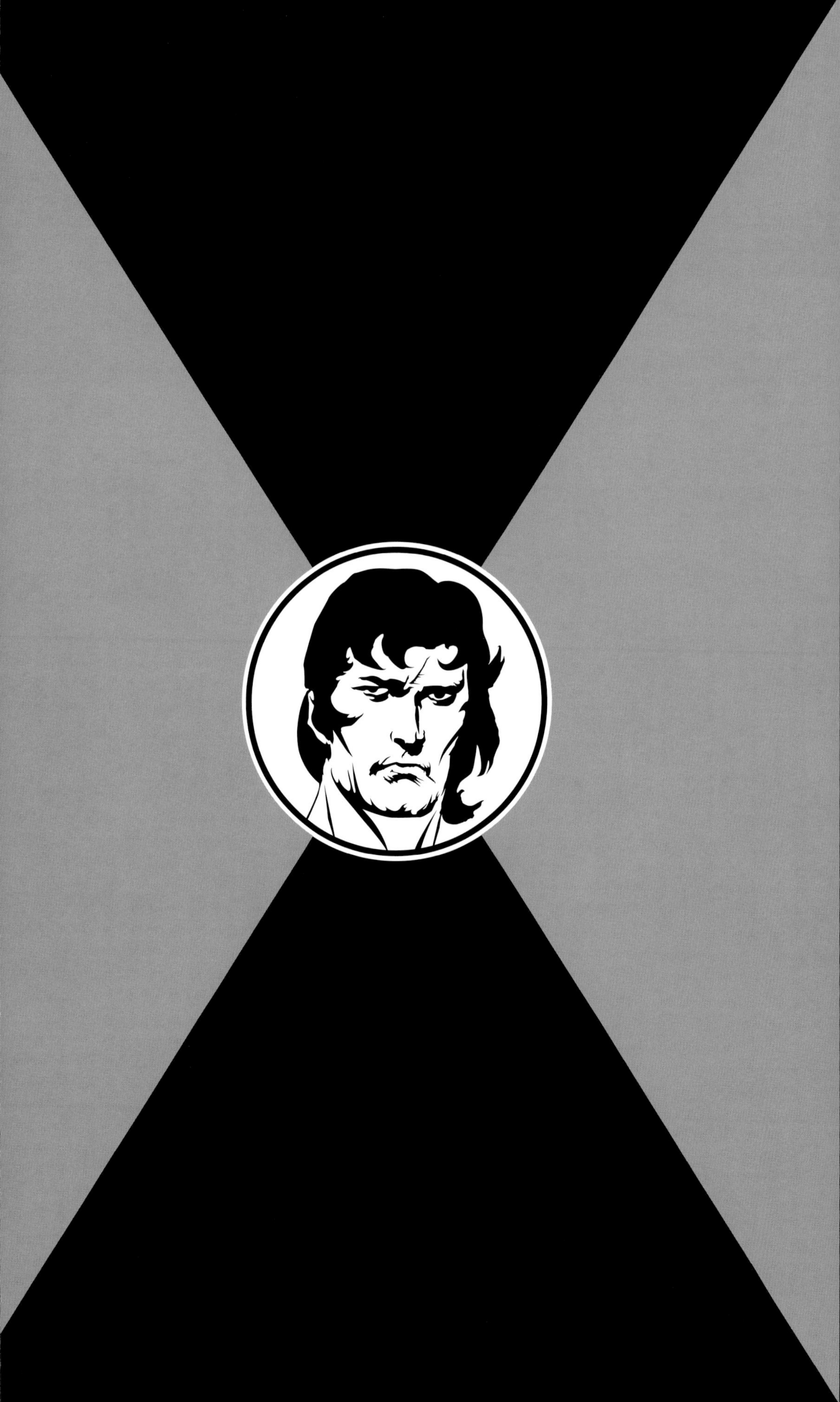

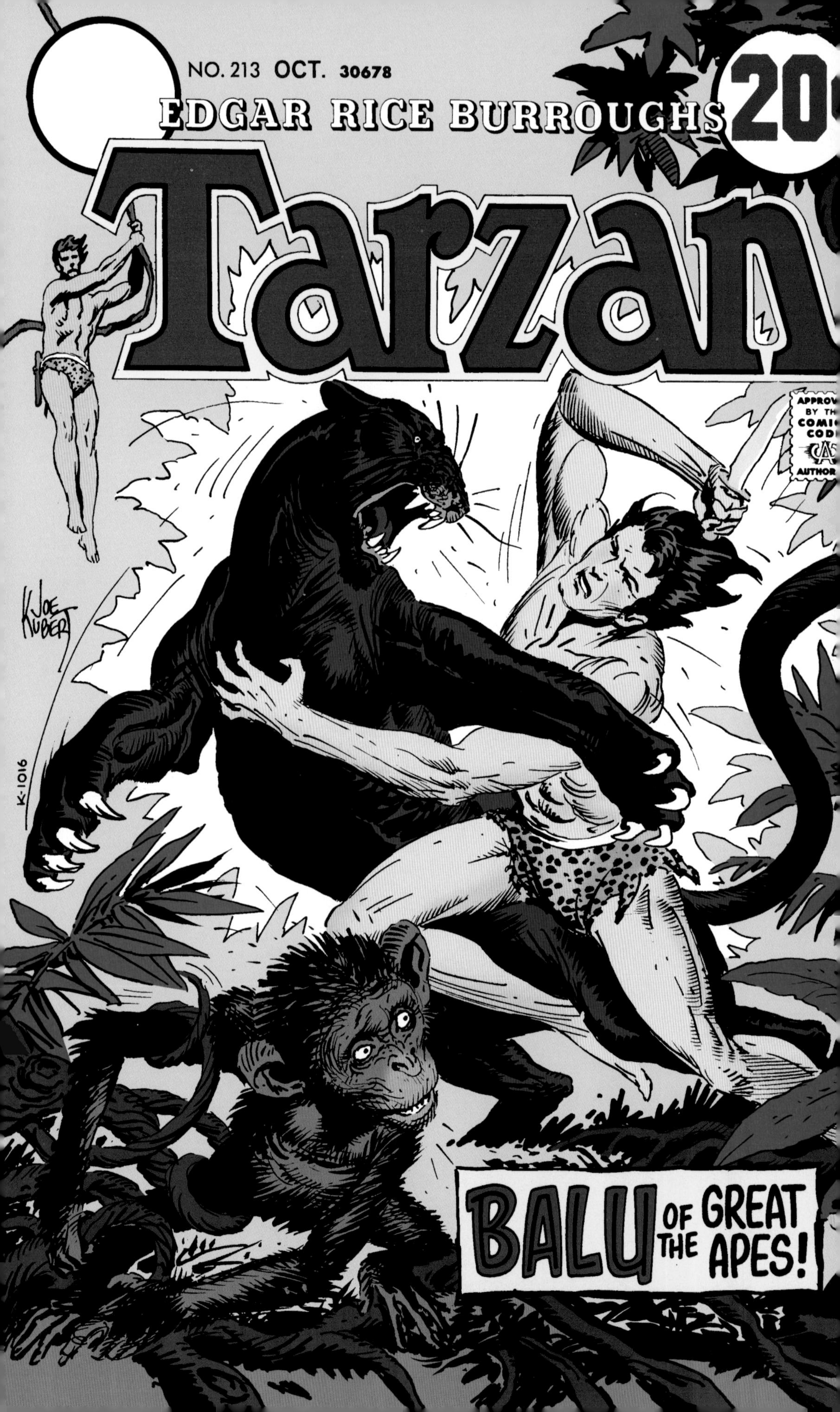
NO. 213 OCT. 30678
20
EDGAR RICE BURROUGHS
TARZAN
JOE KUBERT
K-1016
BALU OF THE GREAT APES!

"*TEEKA...IT IS GOOD YOUR BALU HAS COME! TAUG, YOUR MATE, WILL BE PLEASED...*"

BUT-- THE PLAYMATE AND FRIEND OF HIS YOUNGER DAYS SNARLS IN ANGER...

"*GO AWAY... DO NOT COME NEAR THE BALU! OR I WILL KILL YOU!*"

THE EQUATORIAL SUN FILTERS DOWN THROUGH BLUE-GREEN WEBS OF JUNGLE VEGETATION... AS *TARZAN* RETURNS FROM A PROLONGED HUNT IN THE FOREST'S DEEPEST RECESSES...

K-1017

161

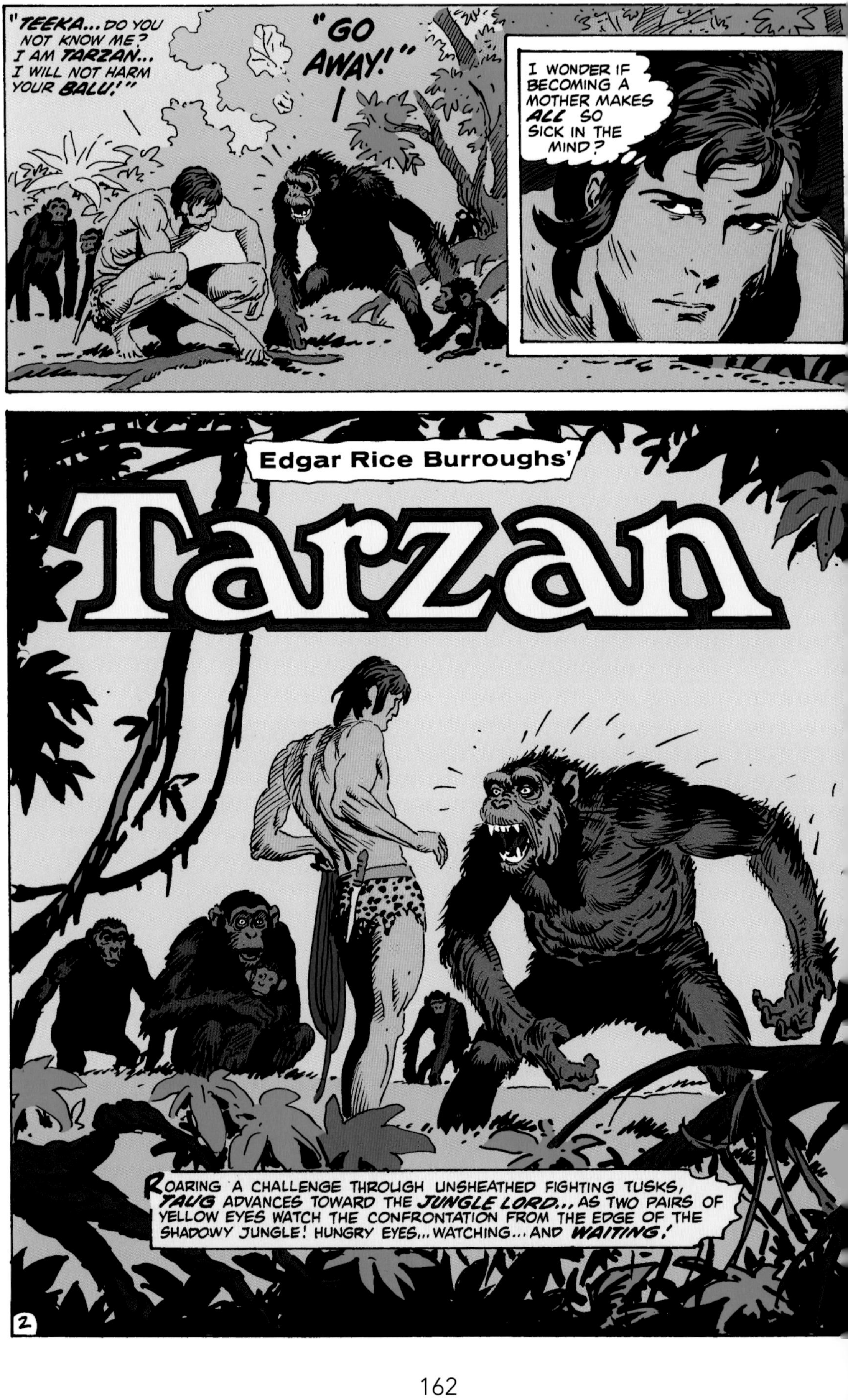
"TEEKA... DO YOU NOT KNOW ME? I AM TARZAN... I WILL NOT HARM YOUR BALU!"
"GO AWAY!"
I WONDER IF BECOMING A MOTHER MAKES ALL SO SICK IN THE MIND?
Edgar Rice Burroughs'
Tarzan
ROARING A CHALLENGE THROUGH UNSHEATHED FIGHTING TUSKS, TAUG ADVANCES TOWARD THE JUNGLE LORD... AS TWO PAIRS OF YELLOW EYES WATCH THE CONFRONTATION FROM THE EDGE OF THE SHADOWY JUNGLE! HUNGRY EYES... WATCHING... AND WAITING!
2

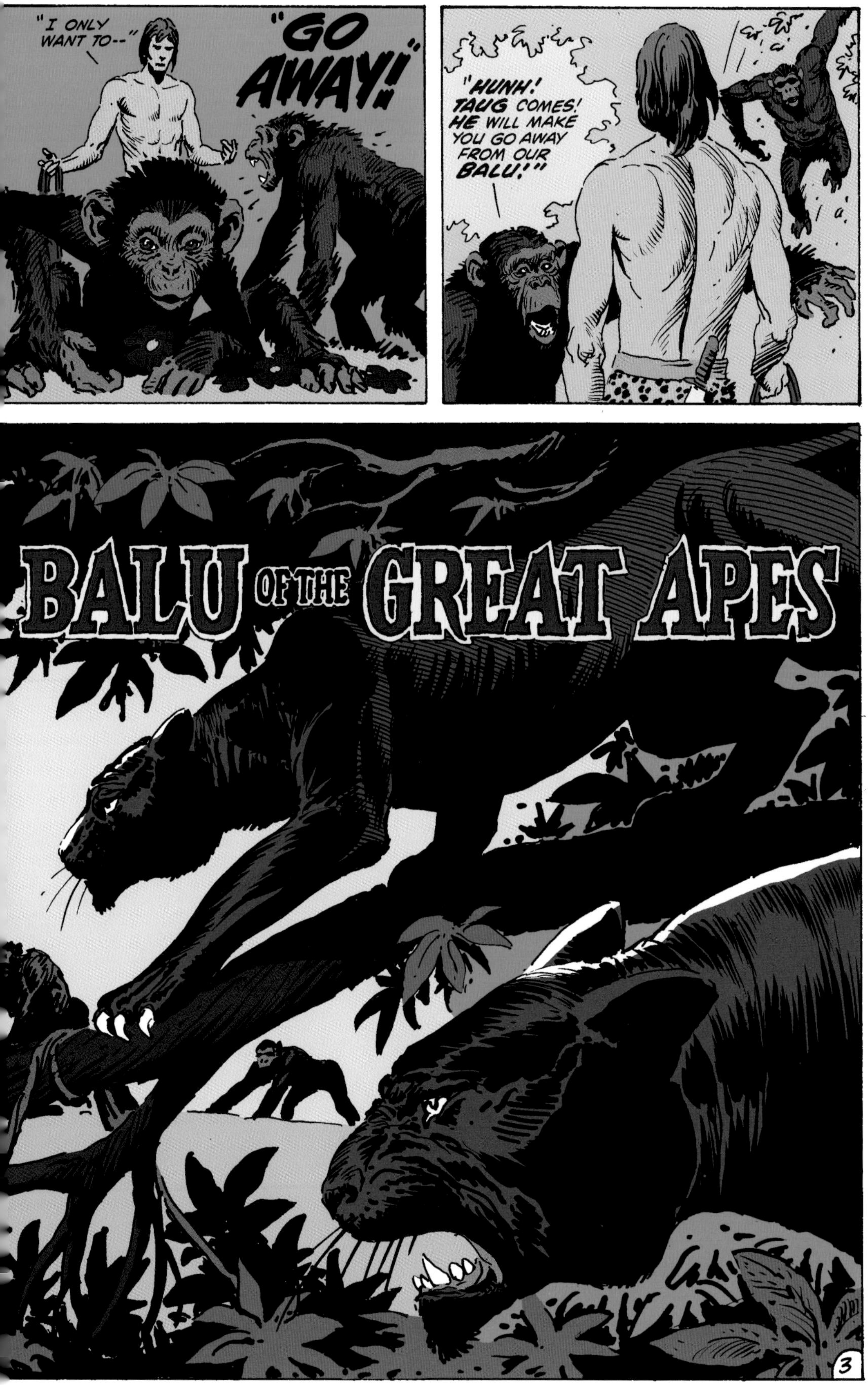
"I ONLY WANT TO--"
"GO AWAY!"
"HUNH! TAUG COMES! HE WILL MAKE YOU GO AWAY FROM OUR BALU!"
BALU OF THE GREAT APES
3

"I HAVE NO WISH TO FIGHT YOU, *TAUG*... YOU ARE MY BROTHER!"

"*TARZAN* WOULD NOT GO AWAY FROM THE *BALU*..."

"*TAUG* WILL *KILL TARZAN!*"

WITH A HIDEOUS SCREAM, THE BULL-APE'S POWERFUL ARM SHOOTS OUT...

SHARP TALONS RAKE THE *APE-MAN'S* SHOULDER...

TARZAN'S FIRST IMPULSE IS TO REPAY HIS ATTACKER IN KIND... BUT...

I... *CANNOT* FIGHT *TAUG!* HE ONLY DEFENDS HIS *BALU!*

"LOOK... SEE THE MIGHTY *TARZAN* RUN FROM BATTLE?"

AND FROM THE DARK JUNGLE, TWO PAIRS OF YELLOW EYES WATCH... AND WAIT...

TARZAN'S ATTEMPT TO AVOID BATTLE INFURIATES *TAUG* ALL THE MORE...

"YOU WILL *NOT* ESCAPE ME SO EASILY... *COWARD!*"

"YOUR ROPE-VINE CAN-NOT HELP YOU..."

THE UNBLINKING, YELLOW ORBS CONTINUE TO STARE... *AND WAIT...*

5

165

BEFORE *TAUG* CAN REALIZE WHAT HAS HAPPENED... HE IS DRAWN SKYWARD... AS *TARZAN* DESCENDS PAST HIM!

"YOU ARE *STUPID*... LIKE *BUTO*, THE RHINO! YOU MAY STAY HERE..."

"GO *AWAY!* LOOK WHAT YOU HAVE DONE TO *TAUG!* HE IS IN *PAIN!*"

SOME OF THE TRIBE'S YOUNG MALES DECIDE TO TAKE ADVANTAGE OF *TAUG'S* SITUATION...

AND *STILL* THEY WATCH...

"YOU HAVE BEATEN AND ABUSED YOUNG AND OLD, TAUG... NOW IT IS YOUR TURN!"

"HIT HIM AGAIN, KARTOOG!"

TARZAN DID NOT MEAN FOR TAUG TO BE MOLESTED! LIKE AN UNLOOSED ARROW HE FLIES UPWARDS...

"YOU ARE MORE TROUBLE THAN YOU ARE WORTH, TAUG! I WILL RELEASE YOU..."

BUT BEFORE TARZAN CAN RELEASE TAUG, THE APE WHICH TARZAN HAD DISLODGED COMES ROARING BACK AT THE APE-MAN...BENT ON VENGEANCE!

AND STILL THEY WAIT...

"KARTOOG DOES NOT PLAY... KARTOOG WILL **KILL** TARZAN!"

"DO NOT TEST ME, KARTOOG... TARZAN IS IN NO MOOD TO PLAY!"

NOW, THE *JUNGLE LORD'S* DEMEANOR CHANGES...ALL SEMBLANCE OF MAN DISAPPEARS...AND A BRUTE-BEAST GLARES AT THE ADVANCING APE!

ERUPTING ACROSS SPACE, *TARZAN* EXPLODES INTO HIS ATTACKER....

WITH INFINITE PATIENCE, THE ONLOOKERS WATCH... AND BIDE THEIR TIME...

TURNING FROM HER *BALU,* *TEEKA* CHATTERS A REPRIMAND AT THE *JUNGLE LORD...*

"NOW SEE WHAT YOU HAVE DONE? *KARTOOG* IS *DEAD....!"*

"LET *TAUG* GO...BEFORE THERE IS *MORE* TROUBLE! HUNH...IF IT WERE NOT FOR YOU MALES... THINGS WOULD BE SO *PEACE-FUL!"*

WHILE TWO PAIRS OF YELLOW EYES FASTEN ON THE UNTENDED *BALU!* AND, NOW...*THEY ACT!*

MOVING IN SILENT, FLUID MOTION... *SHEETA* AND HIS MATE PAD FROM THEIR JUNGLE HIDING... TO STALK THE UNPROTECTED *BALU!*

HIGH OVERHEAD...AS IF ALERTED BY A SIXTH SENSE... THE *APE-MAN* CATCHES SIGHT OF THE *PANTHERS!*

"DANGER!... LOOK TO THE BALU...IT IS SHEETA!"

THE TWO FELINES WILL *NOT* GIVE UP A NEAR MEAL SO EASILY!

CIRCLING THE *BALU,* THE SNARLING CATS BALK THE APPROACH OF THE GREAT APES...

11

171

UNSEEN BY THE TWO THREATENING CATS, A BLACK-MANED THUNDERBOLT DROPS SWIFTLY TO THE GROUND BELOW...

...AND LANDS LIGHTLY BESIDE THE FRIGHTENED *BALU!*

"I AM *TARZAN* OF THE APES...NOT A HELPLESS *BALU!* FIGHT ME IF YOU DARE!"

HAD *SHEETA* BEEN ALONE HE MIGHT HAVE FLED THE *APE-MAN'S* CHALLENGE! BUT--*SHEETA* IS *NOT* ALONE!

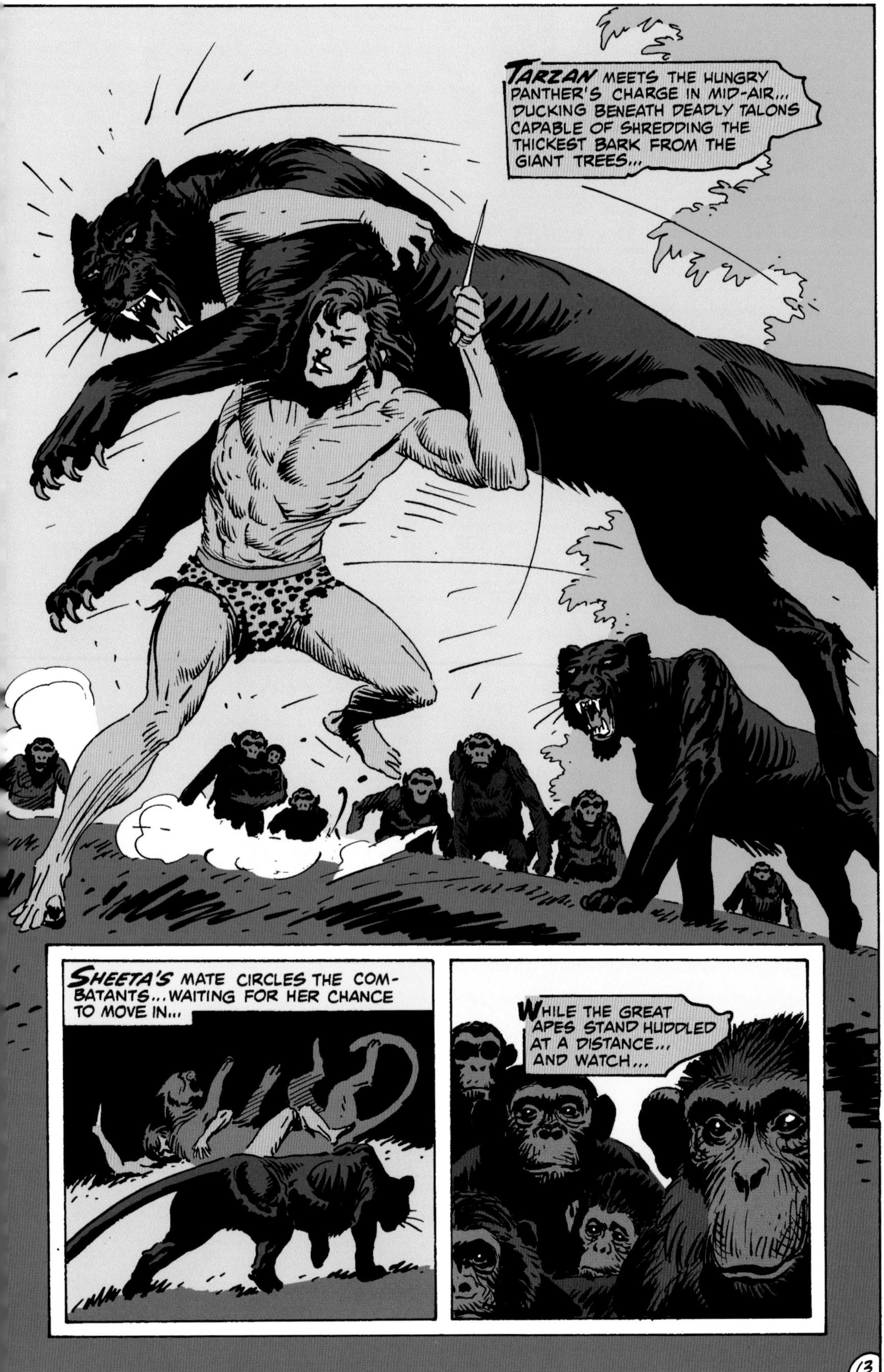
TARZAN MEETS THE HUNGRY PANTHER'S CHARGE IN MID-AIR... DUCKING BENEATH DEADLY TALONS CAPABLE OF SHREDDING THE THICKEST BARK FROM THE GIANT TREES...
SHEETA'S MATE CIRCLES THE COM-BATANTS...WAITING FOR HER CHANCE TO MOVE IN...
WHILE THE GREAT APES STAND HUDDLED AT A DISTANCE... AND WATCH...
13

OVER AND OVER ROLLS *SHEETA*... SCREAMING, BITING, CLAWING... IN AN EFFORT TO DISLODGE THE DEVIL ON HIS BACK!

THEN... *SHEETA* LAY STILL... WHILE THE TORN AND BLOODY *JUNGLE LORD* PAINFULLY TRIES TO SET HIMSELF FOR THE NEXT ASSAULT!

SHEETA'S MATE WILL *NOT* WAIT... SHE CAN ALMOST TASTE THE *APE-MAN'S* FLESH NOW...

"HUNH... BLACK SPAWN OF EVIL... YOU MUST FACE *US* FIRST, IF YOU WISH TO KILL OUR *KING!*"

FINDING HERSELF HEMMED IN BY THE TRIBE OF *GREAT APES*, THE PANTHER ATTEMPTS TO RUN... ONLY TO BE STOPPED AT EVERY TURN BY RAGING SIMIANS SWINGING HEAVY CLUBS WITH *DEADLY ACCURACY!*

NOW... A BLOOD-LUST FRENZY SEIZES THE TRIBE... AND *SHEETA'S* MATE SOON JOINS HIM IN PERMANENT REPOSE!

UNSTEADILY, THE **KING OF THE APES** RISES...

"WE HAVE SLAIN **SHEETA'S** MATE... NO MORE WILL OUR **BALUS** BE STOLEN!"

STILL... MY OWN BROTHERS TREAT **ME** AS IF... I WERE **SHEETA!** EVEN **TEEKA** WOULD NOT... LET ME NEAR HER **BALU**...

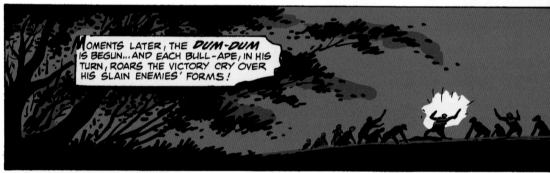

MOMENTS LATER, THE **DUM-DUM** IS BEGUN... AND EACH BULL-APE, IN HIS TURN, ROARS THE VICTORY CRY OVER HIS SLAIN ENEMIES' FORMS!

THE GREAT APES LOOK TO THEIR KING...WHO HAS NOT YET TAKEN PART IN THE RITUAL...

TARZAN TURNS... AND WALKS AWAY!

IN THE DEEPEST PART OF THE DENSE FOREST... A PLACE KNOWN ONLY TO *TARZAN*... THE APE-MAN PONDERS HIS LIFE AMONG THE GREAT APES! AND OF HIS FUTURE...

EVEN THE SMALLEST FISH HAVE THEIR *BALU*... WHILE I, *KING OF THE APES*... HAVE *NOTHING* OF MY OWN!

MUST I BE ALONE... ALWAYS?

IF IT *MUST* BE SO... THEN--*LET IT BE!*

HIS WOUND HEALED, *TARZAN* RETURNS TO THE GREAT APES!

17

177

EYES CAST ASIDE, *TARZAN* DOES NOT EVEN GLANCE IN *TEEKA'S* DIRECTION...

SUDDENLY, A FURRY BALL OF CHATTERING GLEE LEAPS INTO THE *JUNGLE LORD'S* ARMS...

"YOU ARE *TARZAN*, THE GREAT HUNTER OUR KING! IF IT WERE NOT FOR YOU...OUR *BALU* WOULD BE DEAD!"

AND SO, THE *KING OF THE APES* COMES TO KNOW THE HAPPY REWARD OF A GRATEFUL TRIBE...

The End

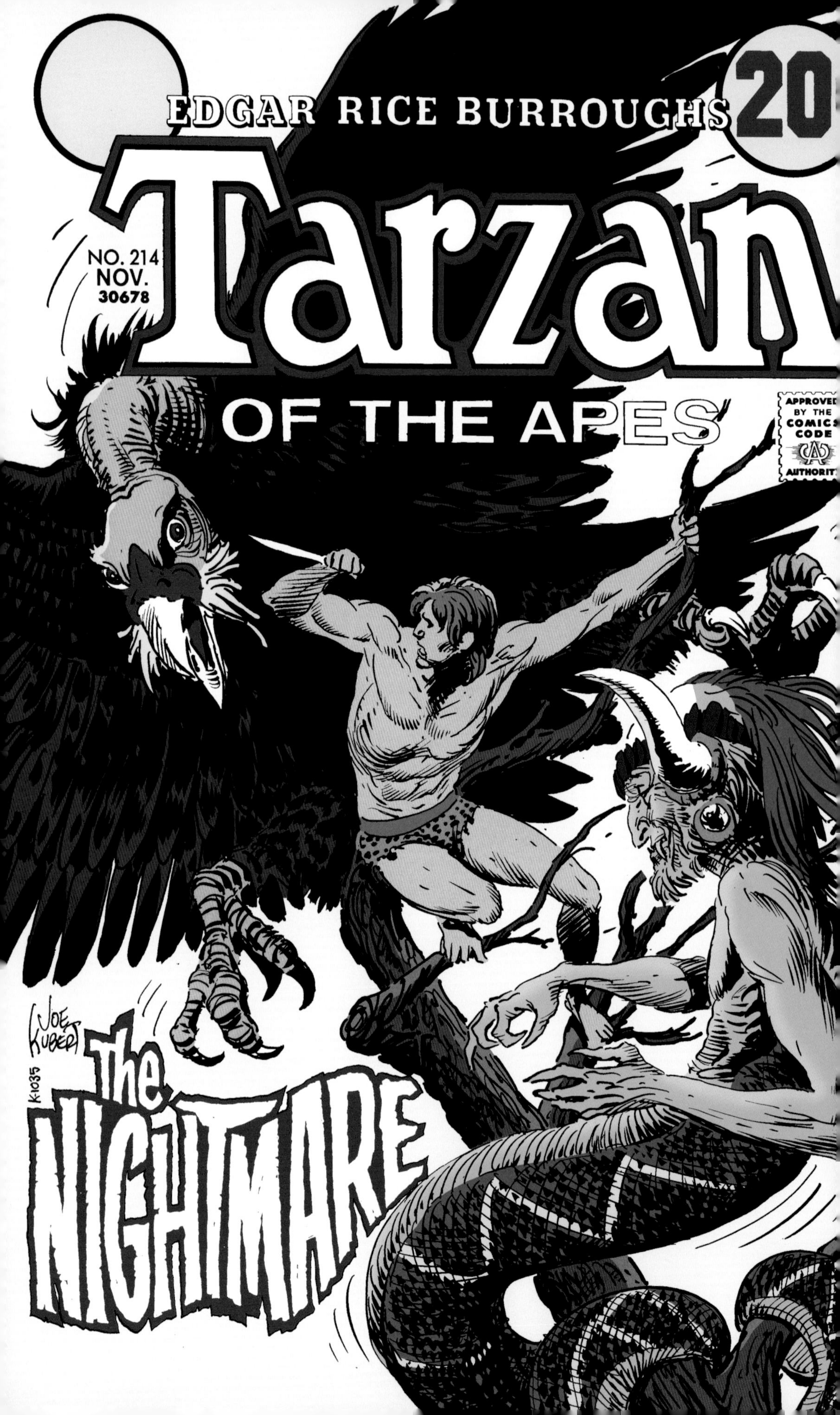
EDGAR RICE BURROUGHS
20
Tarzan
NO. 214
NOV.
30678
OF THE APES
APPROVED BY THE COMICS CODE AUTHORITY
JOE KUBERT
K-1035
the NIGHTMARE

DAY OR NIGHT, *HUNGER* IS EVERY JUNGLE DWELLER'S CONSTANT COMPANION... AND INSISTS ON BEING *SATISFIED!*

...URED BY TENDER GRASSES... ...NERVES TAUT... THE YOUNG *WAPPI* ...AS WANDERED FROM THE FOLD ...NTO THE DARK FOREST...

JOE KUBERT

-1036

SUDDENLY...

HUNH... *TARZAN'S* BELLY WANTS FOR FOOD! BUT-- YOU ARE TOO SKINNY! AND... TOO YOUNG!

RUN BACK TO YOUR *KALU!*

...S THE FRIGHTENED ANTELOPE BOUNDS AWAY, *TARZAN'S* ACUTE SENSE OF SMELL DETECTS THE FAINT ODOR OF *MEAT*... COOKING... FROM THE VILLAGE OF THE *GO-MANGANI!*

1

SWIFTLY, THE *APE-MAN* SPEEDS THROUGH THE INKY BLACKNESS OF JUNGLE NIGHT... BECKONED BY THE RICH SCENT OF FOOD!

THEY WILL NOT MIND ANOTHER GUEST TO FEED... AFTER *THEY* HAVE EATEN SO WELL!

Tarzan

UNERRINGLY, THE *LORD OF THE JUNGLE* LOCATES THE SOURCE OF THE PUNGENT ODORS...

THE *GOMANGANI* EAT WELL! THEN-- WHY SHOULD *TARZAN* GO HUNGRY?

TARZAN KNOWS THAT ONCE THE ORGY OF EATING AND DRINKING IS DONE... THE NATIVES WILL SLEEP HEAVILY! SO... LIKE A SILENT SHADOW IN THE TREE-TOPS... HE CROUCHES AND WAITS!

"THE NIGHTMARE!"

③

FOR DAYS, THE **GOMANGANI** HUNTERS HAD BEEN UNSUCCESSFUL... UNTIL A SHORT WHILE AGO! A SICK WATER BUFFALO FELL VICTIM TO THEIR POISON ARROWS.... AND THE VILLAGERS CELEBRATE BY EATING AND DRINKING THEMSELVES INTO A STUPOR!

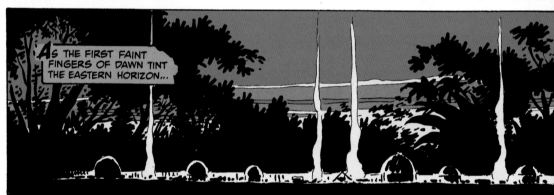

AS THE FIRST FAINT FINGERS OF DAWN TINT THE EASTERN HORIZON...

ONLY ONE FURTIVE FIGURE STIRS... MOVING FROM KETTLE TO POT...

HUNH! THERE IS SOMETHING... AT THE BOTTOM...

TARZAN IS AT ONCE REPELLED...AND SICKENED BY THE TASTE! FOR THE FIRST TIME, THE APE-MAN IS EATING COOKED MEAT! IT DISGUSTS HIM...BUT--HE IS HUNGRY! AND... HE EATS!

A MOVEMENT CATCHES TARZAN'S EYE...

...H...I GROW OLD! I... CANNOT DRINK THE ROOT... AS IN MY YOUTH! MY HEAD SPINS!

I... EVEN IMAGINE... I SEE THE WOODS DEMON... SCRAPING OUR POTS!

I... MUST SLEEP... SOME MORE...

THE OLD MAN WILL NEVER KNOW HOW CLOSE HE CAME TO SLEEPING... PERMANENTLY!

5

185

WITH THE SCRAP OF GREASY MEAT STILL CLUTCHED IN HIS HAND, *TARZAN* ASCENDS INTO THE TOP-MOST BRANCHES OF THE TALLEST TREE...

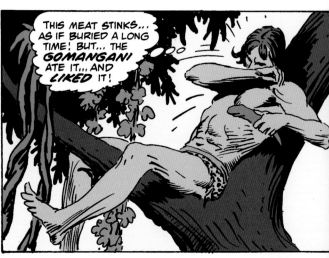

THIS MEAT STINKS... AS IF BURIED A LONG TIME! BUT... THE *GOMANGANI* ATE IT... AND *LIKED* IT!

PFAH... I CAN EAT NO MORE!

HUNH.!... MY BELLY FEELS AS IF... THE MEAT... WILL EAT ITS WAY OUT!

BUT-- I WILL NOT GIVE IT UP SO *EASILY!*

I... I WILL REST...

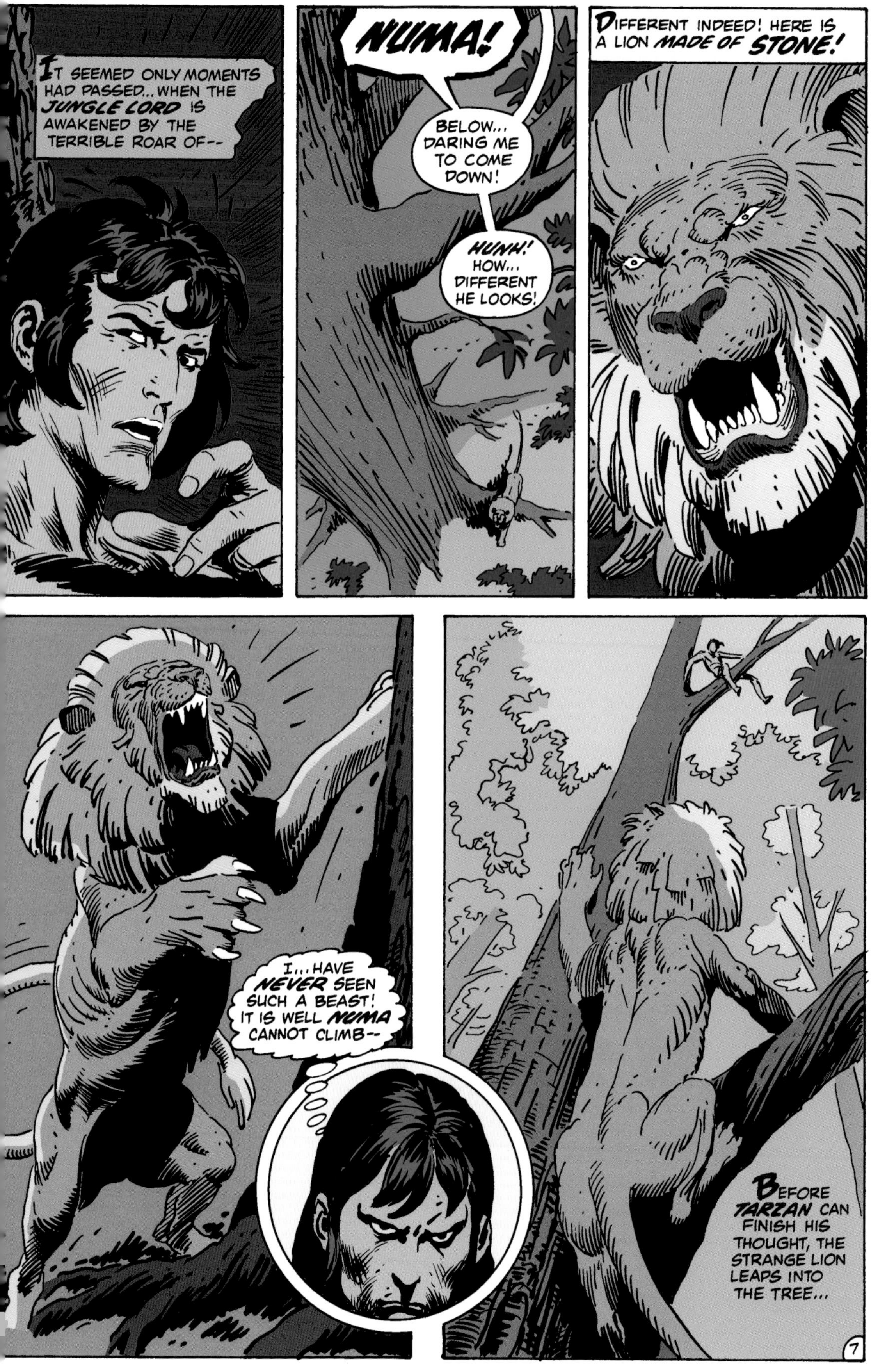

IT SEEMED ONLY MOMENTS HAD PASSED... WHEN THE JUNGLE LORD IS AWAKENED BY THE TERRIBLE ROAR OF--
NUMA!
BELOW... DARING ME TO COME DOWN!
HUNH! HOW... DIFFERENT HE LOOKS!
DIFFERENT INDEED! HERE IS A LION MADE OF STONE!
I... HAVE NEVER SEEN SUCH A BEAST! IT IS WELL NUMA CANNOT CLIMB--
BEFORE TARZAN CAN FINISH HIS THOUGHT, THE STRANGE LION LEAPS INTO THE TREE...
7

Steadily... relentlessly... the snarling beast follows TARZAN up... UP... UP... into the tree's slenderest, swaying branches!

Suddenly... the sky grows dark! There is heard the swoosh of giant wings...

IT... SQUEEZES MY BELLY... TO A *PULP!*

Higher and higher wheels the great bird... until the jungle below looks like a smooth, green carpet!

WHAT... *HAPPENED?* HOW WAS I NOT KILLED... FROM SUCH A FALL?

WHERE DID... SUCH ANIMALS COME FROM?

AND... WHERE DID... THEY *GO?*

THE BIRD... IS *GONE!*

AND THE STRANGE *NUMA*... HAS ALSO FLED!

OR -- WERE THEY EVER *REALLY HERE?*

9

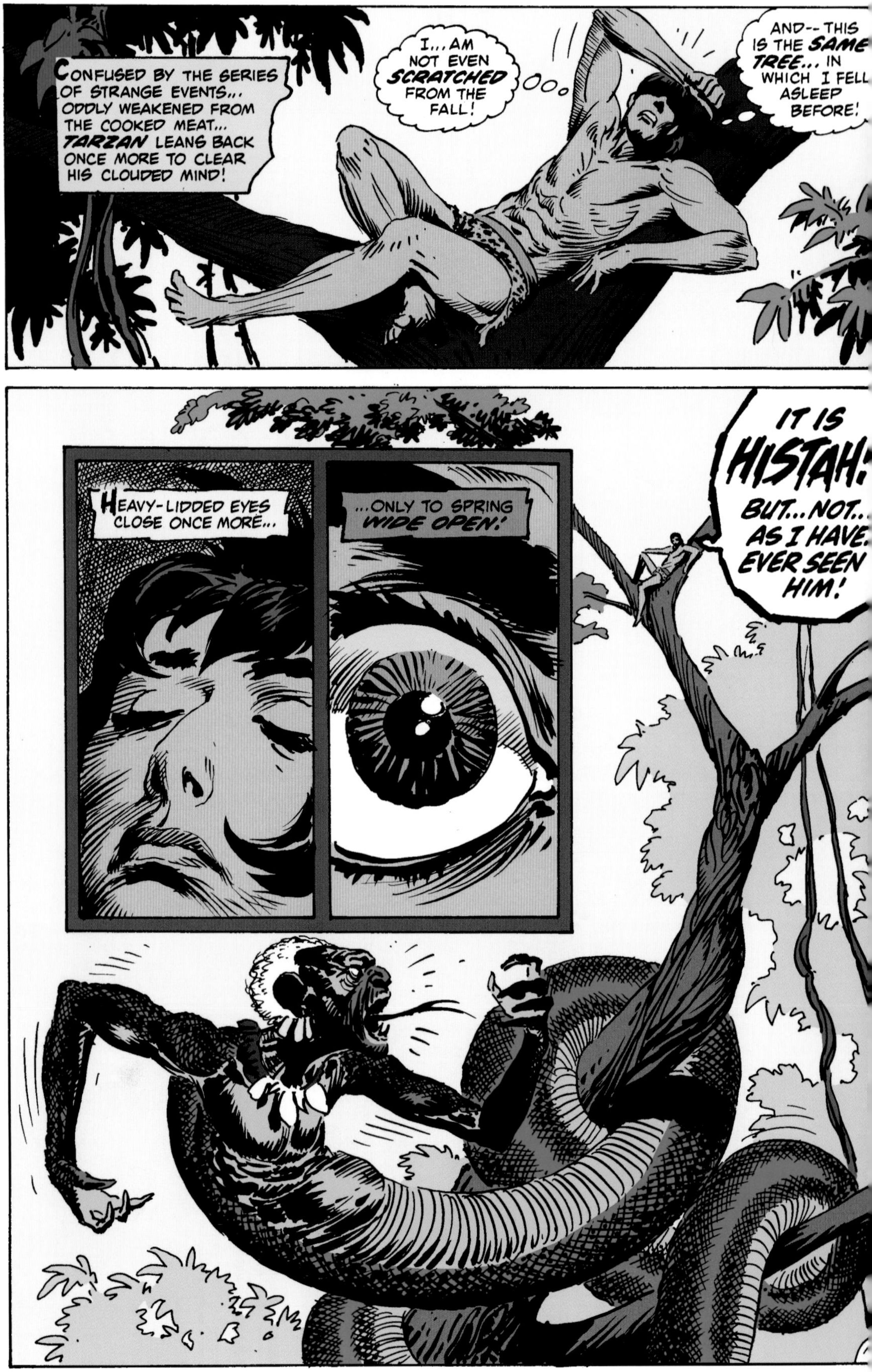
CONFUSED BY THE SERIES OF STRANGE EVENTS... ODDLY WEAKENED FROM THE COOKED MEAT... TARZAN LEANS BACK ONCE MORE TO CLEAR HIS CLOUDED MIND!
I... AM NOT EVEN SCRATCHED FROM THE FALL!
AND-- THIS IS THE SAME TREE... IN WHICH I FELL ASLEEP BEFORE!
HEAVY-LIDDED EYES CLOSE ONCE MORE...
...ONLY TO SPRING WIDE OPEN!
IT IS HISTAH! BUT... NOT... AS I HAVE EVER SEEN HIM!

HISTAH... WITH THE HEAD OF A *GOMANGANI!*

TASTE *MY* TOOTH, *HISTAH!*

HUNH! THERE... IS *NOTHING!*

PROPELLED BY HIS OWN MOMENTUM, *TARZAN* FALLS FORWARD...

INSTINCTIVELY, HIS FINGERS GRIP A TWISTED VINE...

HISTAH! WH-WHERE... DID HE GO?

ONLY... A SMALL *LIZARD...* ON MY ARM!

11

SLOWLY, THE *APE-MAN* DESCENDS TO THE FOREST FLOOR...

MY HEAD... SPINS...

I WILL GO...TO MY NEST... BY THE BIG WATER!

SOON, *TARZAN* APPROACHES THE CABIN FROM WHICH *KALA* (HIS FOSTER APE-MOTHER) SAVED HIM...AFTER *KERCHAK* SLEW THE CHILD'S FATHER, *LORD GREYSTOKE!*

INSIDE...

I WILL...TRY TO LOOK AT... THE BUNDLES OF LEAVES!

THERE... IS THE STRANGE STONE *NUMA!*

AND THE *GIANT BIRD!*

THEN... THEY WERE *NOT REAL!* LIKE THESE FLAT FIGURES ON THE LEAVES... *NOT REAL!*

As THE EQUATORIAL NIGHT LAYS ITS SOFT SHADOWY BLANKET OVER THE JUNGLE...

THEY WERE NOT REAL,...ONLY IN MY *MIND!*

THINGS I COULD NOT TOUCH, AS *THEY* COULD NOT TOUCH *ME!*

...E GOMANGANI'S FOOD... MADE A PAIN IN MY BELLY! AND WHEN I *SLEPT*... I SAW THINGS ...*THAT WERE NOT THERE!*

JUST LIKE THE FORM I SEE IN THE WATER!

IT IS *THERE*... YET IT IS *NOT!*

BUT *I* AM REAL.... AS THE *WATER*... THE *GRASS*... THE *JUNGLE-FOREST!*

*W*EARILY, *TARZAN* LAY BACK... CLOSED HIS EYES ...AND *THEN*--

THE SNAP OF A DRY TWIG!

SOMETHING STEPS TOWARDS ME!

13

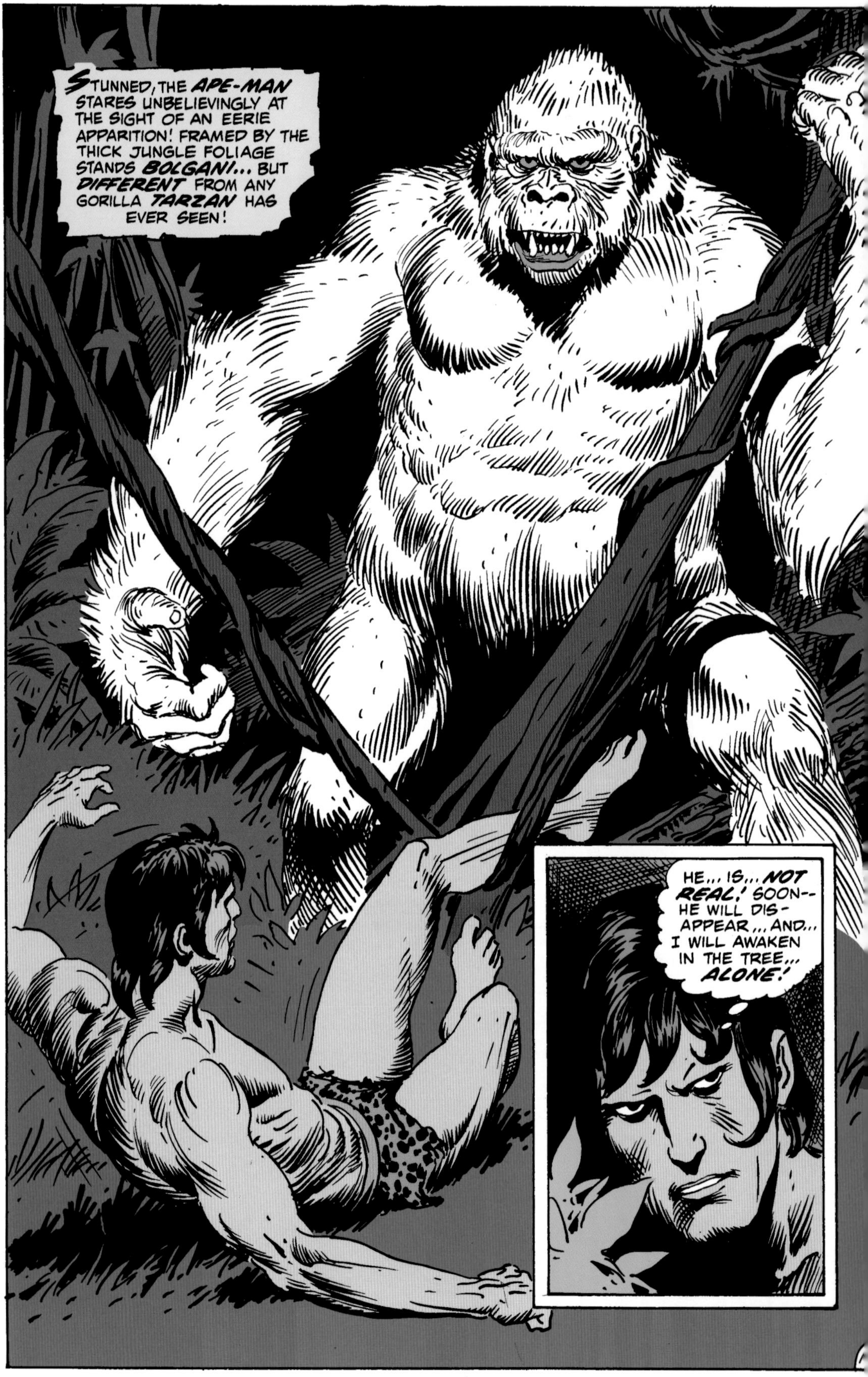
STUNNED, THE APE-MAN STARES UNBELIEVINGLY AT THE SIGHT OF AN EERIE APPARITION! FRAMED BY THE THICK JUNGLE FOLIAGE STANDS BOLGANI... BUT DIFFERENT FROM ANY GORILLA TARZAN HAS EVER SEEN!
HE... IS... NOT REAL! SOON-- HE WILL DIS- APPEAR... AND... I WILL AWAKEN IN THE TREE... ALONE!

...SCREAMS A CHALLENGE AT THE APE-MAN!

FOR A MOMENT, THE COLORLESS BEAST HESITATES... THEN...

I WILL NOT WASTE THE EFFORT OF DOING BATTLE... WITH SOMETHING THAT LIVES *ONLY IN MY MIND!*

GO... AWAY!

YOU... ARE NOT... HERE...

YOU... ARE ONLY... A PIECE OF *SPOILED MEAT...* THAT STICKS IN MY BELLY!

ENRAGED BY *TARZAN'S* PASSIVE ATTITUDE, *BOLGANI* SEIZES HIM IN POWERFUL, CRUSHING WHITE ARMS...

HUNH! WHY... DOES HE NOT... *VANISH?*

LIKE... THE STONE *NUMA*... AND THE STRANGE *HISTAH!*

BOLGANI'S FETID BREATH AND GLEAMING FANGS BRINGS *TARZAN* OUT OF HIS LETHARGY...

WITH A SUDDEN TWIST, THE *APE-MAN* SLIPS UNDER THE GORILLA'S GRASP...

DESPERATELY, THE WHITE *BOLGANI* BACKS INTO A TREE-TRUNK... IN AN ATTEMPT TO DISLODGE HIS NEMESIS...

BUT *TARZAN'S* MUSCLES KNOT LIKE STEEL CORDS... AS THE *LORD OF THE JUNGLE* TIGHTENS HIS STRANGLE-HOLD!

FINALLY-- GASPING FOR LACK OF BREATH-- THE GORILLA SINKS TO THE GROUND... TWITCHES SPASMODICALLY... AND LAYS QUITE STILL...

PLACING A FOOT ON HIS STRICKEN ADVERSARY, THE *APE-MAN* LIFTS HIS FACE TO THE HEAVENS... AND GIVES VENT TO THE *KILL-CRY* OF THE BULL APE!

/7

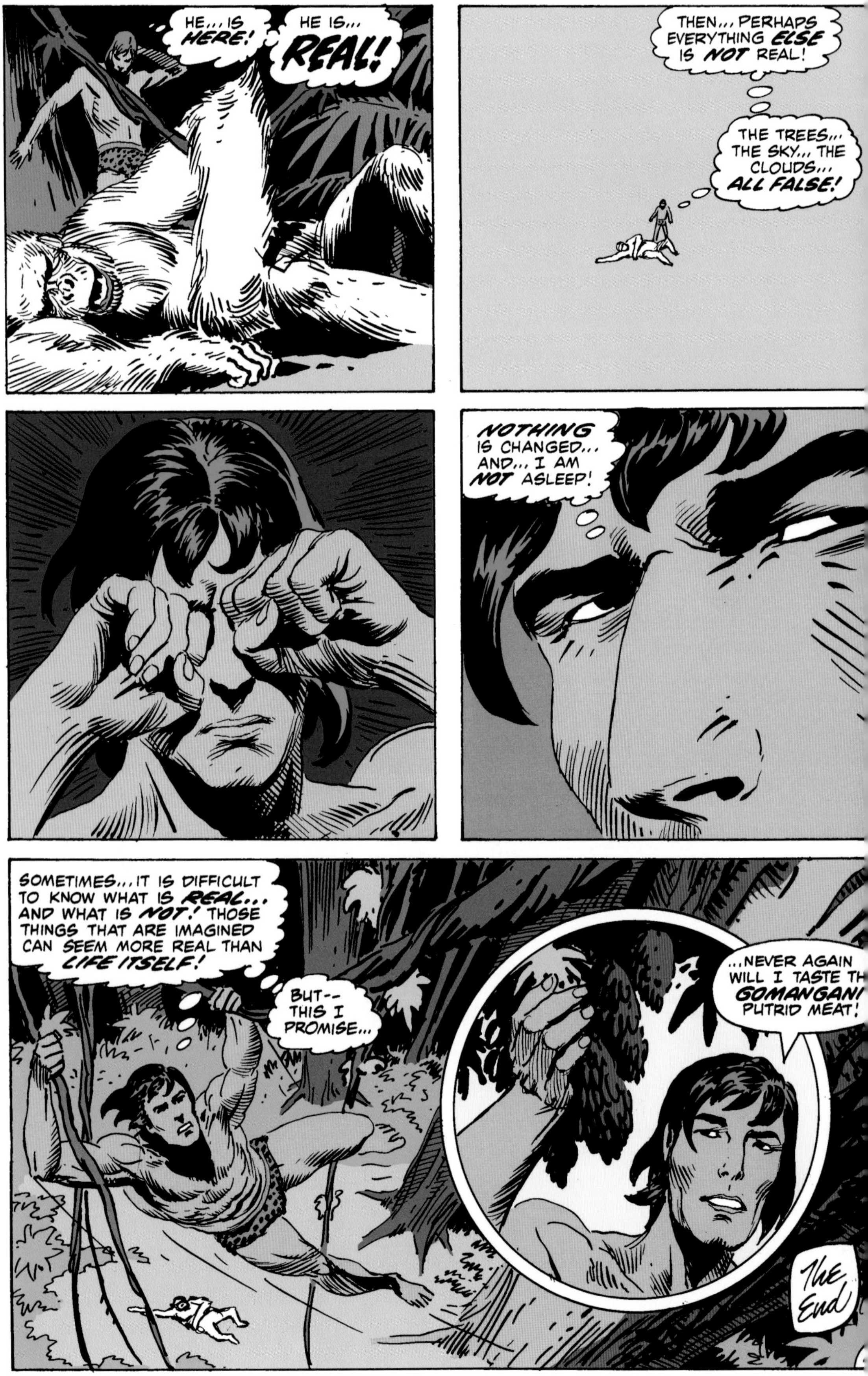
HE... IS HERE!
HE IS... REAL!
THEN... PERHAPS EVERYTHING ELSE IS NOT REAL!
THE TREES... THE SKY... THE CLOUDS... ALL FALSE!
NOTHING IS CHANGED... AND... I AM NOT ASLEEP!
SOMETIMES... IT IS DIFFICULT TO KNOW WHAT IS REAL... AND WHAT IS NOT! THOSE THINGS THAT ARE IMAGINED CAN SEEM MORE REAL THAN LIFE ITSELF!
BUT-- THIS I PROMISE...
...NEVER AGAIN WILL I TASTE TH
GOMANGANI PUTRID MEAT!
The End

CREATOR BIOGRAPHIES

EDGAR RICE BURROUGHS

Edgar Rice Burroughs was born in Chicago on September 1st, 1875, and graduated from the Michigan Military Academy in 1895, where he also served as an instructor. Burroughs wrote his debut novel, *A Princess of Mars*, in 1911, and it first appeared in *All-Story* magazine in 1912. *Tarzan of the Apes* first appeared in the October 1912 issue of *All-Story* and was released as a book in June of 1914 by A.C. McClurg & Co.

In the ensuing years until his death in 1950, Burroughs wrote ninety-one books and a host of short stories and articles. Perhaps best known as the creator of *Tarzan of the Apes* and *John Carter of Mars*, Burroughs' restless imagination knew no bounds, and Tarzan remains one of the best-known literary characters in the world.

JOE KUBERT

Joe Kubert's parents emigrated to the United States from Poland in 1926, when Joe was two or three months old. At age eleven, he began working in the field of comic books as an apprentice for a comics production house. He has worked in the field ever since, and his sixty-five-year history in the medium includes producing memorable stories of such characters as Sgt. Rock, Enemy Ace, Hawkman, Tarzan, Batman, and the Flash. His most recent graphic novels are *Yossel* and *Jew Gangster*. He is currently at work on another graphic novel featuring Sgt. Rock.

Another of Joe's many accomplishments was the founding of the first—and still, only—accredited school devoted solely to the art of cartooning and graphic storytelling. Opened in 1976, The Joe Kubert School of Cartooning and Graphics has produced many of today's leading cartoonists.

Today, Joe and his wife Muriel live in Dover, New Jersey. They have five children and a whole bunch of wonderful grandchildren. Their two youngest children, Adam and Andy, are tops in their field today.